My Dreams Recycled

My journey to turn the divorce lemons
into soul quenching lemonade for millions

TIFFANY ANN
BEVERLIN

Heptagons Publishers
Support@dreamsrecycled.com

Ordering Information:
Quantity sales. Special discounts are available on quantity purchases by corporations, associations, and others. For details, contact the publisher at the email address above.
Orders by U.S. trade bookstores and wholesalers. Please contact us directly.

Printed in the United States of America

Publisher's Cataloging-in-Publication data
Beverlin, Tiffany Ann
My Dreams Recycled / Tiffany Beverlin.
p. cm.
ISBN 978-0-9982686-2-0
1. The main category of the book —Memoir. Other category. 2. Divorce —From one perspective.

First Edition

This book is memoir. It reflects the author's present recollections of experiences over time. Some names and characteristics have been changed, some events have been compressed, and some dialogue has been recreated. Many events and people have been omitted from the book to protect their privacy and also because some people had no or little effect in the authors life's journey. Some occupations, physical properties and identifying characteristics may also have been altered.

Acknowledgements

Firstly I would like to thank, every single visitor to Dreamsrecycled, every follower on every form of social media who embraced my company- every divorcee who kindly shared their personal stories with me. I can't tell you all how much I appreciate you and also have learnt from you. I personally wish you all the happiest of post-divorce lives.

I next would like to thank my three smart, kind and beautiful children, for being such incredible supporters and troupers through my divorce and start of my company. Maxwell who can teach us all about doing your own thing and always with a smile, Griffin who shows the world daily his kindness and compassion and Tilly who is a whirling dervish of creativity and common sense. I am blessed to have these amazing young people call me Mum, you showed me what unconditional love is. Thank you to my parents, who also taught me what love is and who helped where they could in any way they could and who will always be my greatest role models, 50 year marriage and counting. I have no doubt I get my work ethic from my Dad and my empathy and kindness from my Mom. My sister Beth who is an everyday super hero to me and to her patients, defining the word brave and brother David, who has a million genius ideas, who I admire and love both is many ways.

I have a ridiculous amount of people to thank so here goes. Thank you to Nancy. There is no better, more supportive friend I could find. To Dora. There's no more honest, generous-hearted friend you could find, love you ladies. To Michael who I know I could always count on for anything. To Simon you will forever be my FBF. To DD who is a good sport, and Renato who I can never repay for believing in me, who all supported me in my real life, through so many dark days and who kindly allowed me to write about them in this book.

To a wonderful group of friends who I knew had my back, firstly Lois my car pool hero who helped so much with my kids on my worst days. Jennifer, Melissa DD, Rand, Eric, Rebecca, my first helpers who gave so generously of their time and encouragement, who cheered for me. To Julian, many thanks! To Anne, Theresa and Tim my amazing life long British friends, who listened to me moan and made me laugh, even in the darkest hours. I may not have seen you much, but just knowing you were there made everything better. Tim, yes it was all you, I can't lie! To Matt, RIP and I know you would be thrilled for me. Thank you so much for keeping your promise. To My Godmother Aunt Barbara and my Grandmother Lucille, you are both great role models of women in the workforce, love you. To Uncle Bill and Aunt Barbara, thanks for showing me what a loving marriage should be.

Lastly to the person who showed up in my life and made my world instantly brighter and more beautiful. You are my everything. You make me a better person, and you fill my heart daily with pure true love. *Sei il grande amore della mia vita*. You single heartedly showed me what love is. Thank you WJS.

Business thanks

Zach Pardes, who has heard this story far too many times, thank you! Greg Adams, who cleared up everyone else's tech mess, thank you! Elizabeth who I couldn't have asked for better assistant. Renato who always backs me 100%. Steve Williford who patiently awaited this manuscript to edit, and Greg Muse who helped add far too many commas. Thank you. I have a lot to say about everything. Britney Williford for great art design and Michael Cairns whose photography always somehow makes me look amazing! Thank you all from the bottom of my recycled heart!

Table of Contents

Foreword

If you picked up this book, chances are I wrote it for you. Perhaps you are feeling uncertain about your separation, how you will navigate your way through a divorce that lies ahead. Maybe you are divorced and are struggling to find your way out of the grief and sadness that often accompanies it to make your new single life the best life it could ever possibly be. Perhaps you have suffered some other form of adversity in your life, being widowed, laid off, illness.

We unanimously aren't great creatures at dealing with change. I wish in all those instances I could sprinkle fairy dust on everything and fix all the broken, often confused and banged up hearts, but I can't. What I did do though was write this book for you. To point you in the many ways you can recycle your life. The themes are universal; the challenges of recycling your life are often overwhelming for anyone. There are, however, steps we all are capable of taking in our everyday life to help ourselves recover and thrive quicker.

I hope that my story inspires you to have hope for a better future. I hope you learn from my many (and there are many and sometimes humorous) mistakes. I hope you laugh along the way. A sense of humor is I believe a key element of getting through any divorce. Come along with me as I explain, with practical steps that anyone can copy, how I crawled out of the darkest most dismal place of my life, and turned it into a multimillion dollar business.

Sometimes in life all we need is someone to validate what we are feeling and give us hopeful, helpful ways to turn any situation around. This book is filled with these two very things. I receive thousands of messages, emails and texts from divorcees looking for guidance. DreamsRecycled has helped over two million people with their divorces. People asked for this book, and I am a strong believer in sharing your story, to help others, even if parts of this story don't necessarily make me look that great (sorry mom). I wish I had had this kind of book to read when I was going through my divorce. I needed it desperately. Use it as a resource, a companion, a map, and as a friend who gets how terribly awful life can be.

I may not be a doctor or a therapist, but what I am is someone just like you. Thousands have kindly shared their divorce stories, and I want you to know that there is help; there is a better way. You can I totally believe, and as my story proves make your divorce the best darn thing that ever happened to you! You may not feel it right this moment, but it is a very realistic goal to have from divorce or any adversity. You can take these curve balls and use them as spring boards to reach your own personal goals and happiness. Dreams get broken, but this allows us to create new, even bigger ones that ultimately, like mine, will come true! So take a deep breath and come with me as you see how I recycled my dreams!

1

Skinnie Minnie

Where are my pink leggings, mom? . . . Mom!

It's 6 a.m. and my ever-too cheerful daughter Tilly comes racing into my room. She's eight, with a cherubic face, sandy headed, dark-eyed ray of light in what has become for me the darkest of worlds. She is the little girl I always wanted. Yet I was still unprepared for her constant need for attention. She's totally oblivious to the fact that her mom spends 80% of her day confined to her bed. That from the minute she wakes me, I am counting down in my head the seven tasks I must do to get to the point I can get back into bed, or eight tasks, including the finding the pink leggings.

1. Throw some clothes on. 2. Assemble three packed lunches. 3. Throw four egos in toaster. 4. Take Drake, our perpetual puppy, outside. 5. Drive Maxwell and Griffin, my boys, to school. 6. Help Tilly with homework. 7. Drive Tilly to school.

I am not exactly sure when seven simple tasks became monumental mountains to navigate, that took every ounce of energy and every part of my mental capacity to complete. The three previous years had been akin to a macabre tragedy, where everything that could go wrong in the realm of divorce had somehow managed to, and many days I regretted having survived the divorce at all. Luckily, I am a total coward and wouldn't actually harm myself, but there were many days, including this one, that I felt tinges of regret even getting to wake up to yet another day of crushing emotional and physical pain.

Mom hurry up, we are going to be late and don't forget I have Brownies after school!

Her words are literally ringing in my ears as I both attempt to dress, another now difficult task. I stand in front of my mirror as I do every morning, taking inventory of the physical damage my divorce has inflicted upon me. My long dark hair, once shiny and thick, had developed a permanently messy lack-luster that went along with its patches that had grown thin, from stress and vitamin deficiency. My deep brown eyes no longer sparkled, but had sunken into my face enough to exaggerate the size. They oddly showed nothing. No pain, no pleasure, just a vacant hollowness, that only altered when they often spilled with tears, leaving my eye lids far too puffy and sensitive to even contemplate wearing my at one-time signature black eye liner. My body had reverted to a 17-year-old, my arms and legs appearing too long and thin attached to my frame, which also made my movements gangly and less sure-footed. I look at the bruise on my back which has turned a moldy green with a touch of yellow, I really need to see a doctor but with health insurance as one of the many things I lost during my divorce I know I can't. Passing out and in the process hurting myself from the falls can't be normal. In a word, I looked uncomfortable, which in reality was only the tip of the iceberg of misery I felt.

I resist the urge to step on the scale. The last time I had looked, I weighed 103 lbs, which would maybe be okay if I wasn't 5'8". And you could now count my ribs through my skin, front, back and sides. There is mass irony attached to finally reaching and then overshooting your lifetime weight goal. It had been met with a mixed array of both inappropriate comments and envy. My doctor was horrified, my girlfriends weirdly jealous, and my male friends fixated on where my missing 34D breasts had disappeared too.

My breasts were the furthest thing from my mind. My mind just played a never-ending repertoire of thoughts, a list of grievances, unfairness and negativity stemming from my divorce. How had this happened? How had I let this happen? Why did I ever quit my career to be a stay at home mom? How could I have no skills? How could I be unemployable? Why wasn't I living the easy although shallow existence of a "kept" lifetime alimony mom? Sixteen years of marriage - so close yet so far from the 17 required for lifetime alimony in the state of Florida.

Damn Florida, damn the family law system and damn me for being such a wuss, for allowing this to happen. For not forearming and forewarning myself on how divorce works. I naively and very stupidly thought, *Well there must be laws, there must be a system, and of course this is America, the land of justice and fairness and somehow my divorce would just all be OKAY.*

What I hadn't factored in was one key point that would work against me and culminate with me at 103 or less pounds, lying in my bed, not being able to function for EIGHT months.

LIFE ISN'T FAIR

Divorce most certainly isn't when you divorce someone who is self-employed, and you have no access to any financial records or bank accounts for the 16 years you were married. You also most importantly don't understand that as much as we all love our children, giving up your career and work to stay home with them for a decade or more makes you virtually unemployable and unqualified for jobs that would actually be able to support three children.

Task 7 complete for today, I walk back into my 5,000 square foot house that I most certainly can't afford. I see and ignore the ever-growing pile of unopened bills, taunting reminders of my failures, and I run through my head how many dollars I have left till the three credit cards I managed to apply for and have been living on, are maxed out. I stand at the bottom of the steps and again experience the familiar faint feeling - hands tingle, head gets light. It feels like someone is pulling a black shade down over my eyes lids, like an old *Tom and Jerry* cartoon. And that's the last thing I remember, until I wake up, face down on the staircase. I was good this time. I had sat and rested my head on the carpeted stairs the minute I felt the black abyss, as I had named it, coming on. It had become a regular part of my week. It was almost comforting, I had made peace with the abyss for I knew for those few moments I would feel nothing at all, which I welcomed.

I knew it occurred from random texts from my now ex-husband, from debt collector calls, and any time my energy outlay exceeded my energy (food) intake, a mixture of low blood sugar and mind numbing, body destroying stress. I picked up my head and knew I had to find something to choke down. Swallowing was yet another task that had become almost impossible these days. I ran through in my head, if I made coffee and ate something, which also now took almost all my thought processes to complete, that should last until I had to pick up my children, which would require seven Cheez-Its. Seven was all I could ever choke down, so dry and nasty, yet oddly the only thing I ever craved at all during this time.

I crawled back into bed, feeling my hipbones hurting from laying directly on them for 18 hours a day. Even in bed I couldn't get comfortable. I couldn't really sleep, but my bed had become my safe place, the only place that I felt I could cope. I knew I had six hours until school got out and I also knew that for all six of those hours, I would be horizontal, mind racing, tears flowing, controlled by the overwhelming feeling of hopelessness. I also knew that I couldn't live like this much longer, but I had no clue how I would ever get out of bed or this seriously depressed state of mind, one that before my divorce I had never encountered.

As I lay there, I went through my phone. My phone had become my lifeline. It was how I spread the lies and untruths, telling family, friends and acquaintances I was OK. This was easy to do via text. I was never able to speak, petrified that if anyone showed me any human kindness, I would break down in tears, and as a Brit, we prefer to keep a stiff upper lip. Chin up, and all that stuff. I had moved to the USA, to work at Universal studios as a 21-year old bright eyed, bushy tailed optimist. How fun would it be to work in Florida for a year at a theme park and get paid to do it, and spend weekends at the beach! This I had done and loved every single moment of it.

I reluctantly left after my first lovely and rambunctious son, Maxwell, had turned 18 months. He was a blonde, hazel eyed, gorgeous child who also was highly stubborn, and I had found that day cares for theme park employee hours were few and far between. I, of course, as a stay at home mom, thought two kids would be better than one and had my second dark haired, dark eyed pensive beautiful boy, Griffin, two years later. Boys are a handful but they had been unbelievable troupers during divorce. When we sat them down and told them, not only were none of the three shocked, not one shed a tear. They just asked three questions, which I think sums up what is most important to all children:

1. *Are we still living with you?*
2. *Are we still going to the same schools?*
3. *Will we still see Dad?*

That was it. We answered yes to all and they literally went back to playing a video game. To be a kid and be that okay with change. I lay there thinking of my three little heroes and the same thought ran purposely through my head - they deserve a better mother, a more successful one, one who isn't unemployable and can support herself and them too. I didn't want to say no to them for everything. I didn't want them to eat crappy store brand cereal, and I most certainly didn't want them to realize just how terribly sick I had become from my divorce.

I doze off to sleep, realizing that I had, in fact, spent the entire night awake on my phone, researching jobs that I wasn't qualified for, looking at online courses, further education that I couldn't afford, and had less than no interest in, such as pharmacy tech, realtor, or lawyer. Now lawyer would work although who has another two years and tens of thousands of dollars to plough into that? I didn't. As I float in and out of sleep, which is now my favorite activity of the day, I feel nothing. If I am lucky, I have a happy dream. If unlucky, a stress one which tended to happen more to me during the night and yet another reason I preferred to stay awake most of those hours.

Knock, knock. I ignore the intrusion and hope they go away; I am no longer people friendly. *Knock, knock, knock*. It is more urgent and now accompanied with a *Tiffany Tiffany! It's Nancy*. Nancy is one of only four friends I have left after my divorce, and I know her well enough to know she's not leaving until I get up and answer the door. If you ever want to know who your real friends are, get divorced. It's a sure-fire friend sorter. *Tiffany, are you ok? Hello, hello? Answer the door!* I stagger back down the stairs, briefly stopping to contemplate whether I should throw on more clothes or let her see my ribs through my tank top, but she is now banging so much, I want her to stop, so I open the door to her, and brace my ears because I know what is to come.

Nancy and I connected when our children were at pre-school. She was a friend. Nancy is Puerto Rican and proud of it. She is gorgeous, and proud of her curves, and we nick name her *Fancy Nancy* because she would rather die than leave the house without makeup, heels, and her hair done perfectly. She is also one of those people who doesn't take no for an answer. Nor does she have any personal space. She is standing now far too close to me and very animatedly saying what I have heard a hundred other times from her, *What are you doing today? Why don't you get up and eat something? You are a Skinny Minnie, Tiffany! Eat for goodness sake!*

This isn't helping. She seems far too animated, too loud and possesses too much energy, which engulfs me and both makes me feel better and worse all at once. *Go get dressed we are going to lunch. We are meeting Dora, at Press 101.* I try and mutter that I have things to do before she jumps down my throat and says she is waiting there until I go with her. I know from previous times, resistance is pretty much futile against the persistence of Fancy Nancy. I crawl back upstairs, throw on a dress which now fits like a sack and some sandals as I hear her on the phone whispering in her 97% English and 3% Spanish to Dora that we are meeting her and yes, I look even worse than before. I have no makeup on, my hair is a wreck and I totally don't care at all. I brush my teeth, gagging on the toothpaste - such a far jump from the person I was when married, who would always fear running into someone and not looking presentable. I sit in her car and she drives with her lead foot to Press 101, I say barely anything, which is one of the best things about Nancy. She can hold both sides of the conversation and she knows me so well, she can answer herself as well, with barely any participation from me.

Dora greets me with a hug and a "you look like shit." She is the only person in the world who can swear at you in such a way you know she cares deeply for you. "Tiffany, let me do your hair. What are you doing! What if some gorgeous man walks in here and he is supposed to be the love of your life but instead runs away in horror? You really do like shit! Do you even look in the mirror? You look worse than a freakin' troll. Why don't we dye your hair pink and send you back to the 80s?"

I start to laugh. Dora can make anyone laugh. Then she laughs. Then

Nancy laughs, and I realize that I haven't laughed or smiled for weeks. She's a petite, stunning Londoner of Greek decent with probably the best naturally curly hair on this planet. She dresses a cross between rock star and urban hippy and swears more than anyone else on this planet, as only a Londoner can, really. Nancy and Dora are friends-in-law to me. They have, since my divorce, been forced into a kind of tag team of baby sitters and suicide watchers, checking on me via text, or ambushing me for lunches for months now. It's funny how tables turned for all three of us. Each of us was married and they both used to tell me their problems and I would help them. Now they have both become the advisors, the mini-mommies to me, fussing over me, buying me lunch, listening to me cry, texting with me till two in the morning when I just am too afraid to be alone.

We sit with our lunch and the interrogation begins:

Did you get any interviews?

No.

Job prospects?

No.

New lawyer?

No.

Did you get your settlement money?

No.

What are you going to do?

I don't know.

Same conversation, different day. I could see in their eyes the concern, the worry, the love. They had no answers but they listened. Sometimes that's what you need, really, in dire situations. People who care, who listen, who you can tell exactly how bad your life is, and you know they won't judge you or think worse of you. I may not have had a penny to my name, but I had billion dollar friends who took time from their husbands and kids to babysit me. After watching me push around the food on my plate, Dora announces that I should date, *'cause if you have no job, no money, a mass of debt, throwing yourself into online dating is a sure-fire distraction, plus we can help you choose who to date*. I look at them both like they are mad, remind them that I have not dated since the Clinton administration when the only method of communication was a beeper and a landline I shared with my roommate Kathy.

NO NO you have to do this Tiffany! You have been separated forever, it's time, plus what else do you have to do? It will be good for you get out, and eat free food! They drop me at home and as I crawl back in my bed of safety, I open Match.com on my computer and begin window shopping. Who knew so many men enjoy holding fish up and posing in front of the bathroom mirror? This clearly would be a very bizarre arena to navigate and I wasn't sure I was up for the challenge. I wasn't sure I could even last an entire night out in public without passing out, so it seemed very much a large leap for me.

Time came to pick up my children and I was always both relieved to not be alone again and overwhelmed by their activities, homework, tests, school projects and those endless pieces of paper with info about upcoming events that brought fear into all parents that you may drop the ball on one kid, one activity on one day that would confirm to the entire world your worst fear that you really are a horrible, unorganized parent.

Believe me, as a room mom, PTA member and 5th grade party chair, you can be sure everyone in *Parentville* knows who and how the ball was dropped. Forget the Capri suns or cupcakes and you better hang yourself in shame from the closest tree. The best thing about my divorce had ironically been that it had become a *get out of everything* card for me. I clearly wasn't coping well, and teachers, school board members and brownie troop leaders could see the mess I was and stopped asking me to help with anything, leaving me many, many uninterrupted days in bed where I just checked the *no* box on those school volunteer papers and stayed in bed instead of helping with anything.

Maxwell, my oldest son, has a personality like an ever-happy golden retriever; social, bright, gifted and at times lacking in common sense, he needed constant activities and outlets. He was both musical and sporty, so his soccer, orchestra and band practices played a large role in the nightly kid activities. Griffin, thank goodness for me, had quit soccer and was happy to play Wii. Griffin is a middle child like I am, a quiet, kind hearted, thoughtful boy who, since the divorce, had stepped into mini-dad position. He watched out for his little sister and made her food on command if he sensed I had yet another migraine which had become the all-purpose excuse for when I literally couldn't get up to feed them, or I was cooking for them while crying, or was sobbing on the phone, trying to sort out the nightmare that was untangling 16 years of life from my Ex.

Tilly had been so young during our separation that she can't really remember a time properly when we were even married, she's always going to be my baby as the youngest but like many girls these days, she's ridiculously grown up, and independent. She, too, has a perpetually sunny disposition and outgoing demeanor that she uses to socialize with hence the soccer team, Brownies, dance, and choir member activities.

The evening hours were a blur of feeding, mostly frozen easy cheap foods. On nights I really couldn't function at all, activities where shelved and cereal was dinner. I spent most of these school nights trying to get each kid to the correct activity at the correct time. Where possible, I hid in the car or waited in a side room at whatever place they needed to be, on my phone doing a vast array or research. Research on anything or everything I thought may help alleviate this ridiculous situation I found myself in, like somehow my phone held all the answers. Google search was my master, taking me from one dead end realm of thoughts and solutions to another.

I lived for Friday night, knowing that I had weekends with no school runs and only two soccer games. Weekends became a sleep fest for us all. Not much got done. We watched a lot of movies. I switched from being horizontal in my bed to being horizontal on the couch, which the kids seemed to prefer. The kids were all too small to leave ever and I had no desire to leave them or my house anyway, so this is what we did. Movies, chicken nuggets, and Wii. It wasn't a life; it was survival. Any day I lived through, didn't pass out during and had no additional huge set back, i.e. broken AC broken fridge etc., became a small victory, and one I never celebrated but in my own way was grateful for. The never-ending prayers of *just don't let anything else bad happen,* must have somehow on most days been heard.

Some days, though, they weren't, and we relied on the smallest human kindness shown by others to keep me going; a text, a kind word, a show of compassion. People like Vinny from the local garage whom I had taken my beat up broken down car to a million times, and could read the despair on my face, filling my car with power steering fluid for free on a day when I wasn't sure I would survive.

Or the really nice AAA lady who was so horrified that I was without coverage and standing on the side of the road with my three small children, and no working credit cards. The random people who stopped to jump my car, while we sweated to death in the parking lots it so often broke down in. I was incredibly grateful to these people who didn't know me but treated me with this kind of kindness. I was a walking shell of a human and it amazed me how some people so clearly saw it and how most were oblivious to it.

2

Mismatch Marcus

Why are we doing this? No one will want to go out with me, I have no photos, I don't know what I am doing and I haven't dated since the Macarena was in vogue.

My mind wondered to bad 90s music when Shania Twain preached to us that any man of mine better walk the line. If only I had listened to her in 1995 I wouldn't have been in this state.

Dora and Nancy had yet again ambushed me from my bed cocoon and, after making coffee, we were all lined up in front of my laptop, like three naughty imps eager to see what kind of world online dating would be in the fine town of Orlando, home of never ending happiness and tourists running around in ill-fitting but matching Mickey shirts. I was about to embark on a very eye opening journey, one filled with deceit, lies, laughter, excitement, broken promises, misread social cues and enough unsolicited photos of man's junk that I seriously considered life in a convent to avoid them.

Match.com was our first stop. "Let's sign you up!" says Nancy, "There must be some great guys out there. And let's face it, your bar has been set low. "Find someone super-hot, no divorced dads who have let themselves go."

Dora urged, giggling, "Oooh be a cougar! How fun! Date a young hot dude, one who you don't have to talk to, just go out with. Have fun, if you know what I mean."

Still not completely convinced that I should be doing this at all, I responded, "I already have three kids. The last thing I want is to date a fourth man child." "I only date older. Find me someone tall, cute, who travels and is smart."

We set up the quite extensive profile and I realize that I have hardly any photos of me at all. I have never taken a selfie or had a photo shoot. The best I have is a photo in a pool cover up and a photo from a birthday party we cropped to eliminate everyone else. That would have to do, I was a 5.8 brunette, unemployed, stay at home mom. Looking for a fricking miracle, which there was no check box for, so I had to go with professional over 5.10.

There were also sadly no boxes for, rescuer, savior, fixer of everything. Beggars can't be choosers comes to mind. I was looking for someone honest, trustworthy, fun, educated and well-travelled. This didn't seem like an extreme wish list. I refrained from saying anything about me as what was I really going to say?

Messed up, insecure, too thin, mostly depressed unemployable, single mom loser seeks someone who can hug me so tight all my pieces stick back together.

Which is actually what, at the time, I was looking for. A person to fix me, save me and love me. It wouldn't be till much later on that I realized the important life lesson that the only person who can fix or change anyone is himself or herself. Which was - Me.

The profile was up and I had paid some kind of membership fee, which I felt deeply guilty about, spending $39 on finding a man when I couldn't pay my bills. But it seemed like a must-do move at the time. Plus peer pressure. I was partially going along with the online dating plan to fool Nancy and Dora into thinking I was fine or going to be fine, but believe me when I say I was a valley far away from fine on any level.

All of a sudden Nancy decided we needed wine to start our very serious quest for a super man who would save Tiffany! Thus, with alcohol flowing, we immediately began the quest and narrowed down the field of prospects to taller than 5.10, employed, no smoking, drinks only socially, over 40, preferable a parent, and on and on until we were left with 164 men within 50 miles of my home. Well, 164 seems like pretty good odds until, you subtract every single person you are not attracted to, every profile with anyone holding a fish, anyone with a cat, anyone naked in front of their bath room mirror, anyone with profiles with sexual innuendos and word to wise, use spell check. I love music and am a1969Rapper is very different statement than I love music and I am 1969Raper.

Also, it was amazing how many people managed to post photos where in photo one, the person seems attractive and normal, maybe in a business suit, and you are thinking, Ahhh, he seems nice I could date him. However, photo one is followed by a photo of the same guy at a strip club with his face buried in a stripper breasts.

If nothing else, a search through online dating profiles will both horrify you and make you laugh so much that wine snorts out your nose. This wine snorting is amplified when you have two funny, happily married friends, commenting on the prospects like a combination of man pushers and match makers gone awry.

Look at his arms is quickly followed with but look at how filthy his bathroom is! You can't date him may get staph infection from the house. Or, He seems nice. See, there is a photo with his mom. But this is followed with, But who uses a photo of their mom to get laid?

Every photo and every word was triple analyzed by us and in the end of that session there were a lonely pitiful four men. What we didn't realize was that as we were looking at men, it was alerting them that I had viewed them, and as I was new meat and apparently somewhat attractive, my inbox began to fill.

Ever had a new toy? Match.com quickly became mine. I could lay in my cocoon, browse, read, answer, block, delete and message totally protected by the keyboard force field that we all feel protects us from any reality, as we can say, do, and be anything we want with a few strokes of the keyboard.

I was definitely braver than I appeared via messaging. I was guarded but polite. I was shocked by how many messages I was getting and from not just Orlando but from all over USA. Shockingly, most of them referred to me being beautiful, pretty, stunning or gorgeous. This was very confusing to me. Along with crushing sorrow, my divorce had left me feeling anything but attractive. I couldn't remember being told for decades that I was beautiful, sexy, etc., I actually had very big trepidation that on a dating app, no man might even be attracted to me or think I was pretty. I think this is a very common feeling among both divorced men and women. A feeling of not being good enough, pretty enough or even just not being enough. The seemingly never ending message stream filled with compliments and invitations became my drug of choice; each message started to heal, started to make me seem a little tiny bit more hopeful that there may really be a man who could and would love me. That's when Marcus appeared.

When we had scrolled through countless profiles, we had come across the profile of a 6.4 Texan transplant who quite frankly looked like a cross between Superman and Mr. Big from Sex in the City. In every photo of him, he was in front of a different monument in a foreign country. What wasn't to love about this guy? His summary was filled with commonality. He was an architect, a reader, a lover of literature, a real life renaissance man with a kiss curl and a shy but mischievous grin and I knew I was going to be in trouble the minute I saw a message from him in my inbox.

"Come back! You are the most beautiful girl on here! Don't look and leave!"

What to say? What doesn't sound lame or cheesy or needy or too nonchalant or too eager? I couldn't think what to say but "hi. "Luckily for me that didn't drive him away and we very quickly began a flirting fest that quickly spilled over into text. He was so eloquent and his extensive vocabulary and artistic knowledge was intoxicating to me.

We discussed travelling, life, our children, Shakespeare, Tolstoy and on and on. We spent entire evenings simply texting. One night was spent only texting in naughty Old English. We thought we were funny and that was all that counted. Our brains had bonded in a few short days, and, after a few coffee dates, and a quick sushi lunch, he asked me to dinner on Friday night. Day dates had become the norm as they required no babysitting money. An actual dinner date filled me with fear.

It was a Tuesday and I was filled with fear, uncertainty and insecurity, and I had nothing to wear. Which called for backup in the form of Dora. "Dora do you remember that super-hot guy with all the travel photos? Well I met him and he asked me to dinner Friday night!"

"That's awesome babe, he's going to love you."

"But Dora, I have nothing to wear. Nothing fits and I have no money to buy anything, plus what do you wear on a date? With a hot guy in this decade?" I am totally lost and panicking "

"Do you think you can get your ass out of bed and come here? You can borrow something of mine," she said

"Be there in 20".

I walk into Dora home, filled with laughter and love and I can't help but wonder what it would be like to have that, a loving husband, a supportive best friend you marry, so alien to me. She has her espresso machine going, maybe best coffee you can get from anyone's kitchen, complete with your choice of cinnamon or chocolate sprinkles.

Since my divorce, Dora has become like a sister to me, someone I know beyond a shadow of a doubt would show up whenever needed with anything I needed. She also happens to be an amazing hairstylist and she demands that she does my hair before I get to even look at her clothes.

As I sit in her make shift hair dresser zone in part of her laundry room, I feel waves of something I haven't felt for quite some time, the feeling of looking forward to something, to meeting someone, such a feeling I had forgotten. Dora wants to know all the details of my new friend Marcus and I am happy to share them. I can see less concern in her eyes as she fixes my hair and deems me somewhat presentable to date. She keeps saying same thing, "Happy for you babe! This will be good for you."

I am not sure it will be good for me but I am dedicated to following through. How bad can it be -dinner with a tall Texan? We go into the expansive closet and I notice how pretty and bright and girly everything is and I realize that I have been wearing nothing but workout clothes/pajamas for about a year, I can't even remember wearing a dress or real clothes. In fact, over the course of my long stint of servitude (I mean marriage), I had adopted the very dull, non-sexy, mommy wardrobe of capris and t-shirts. These were deemed best to navigate the never-ending nursing and being spat up or puked on by my three children, one of which I am pretty sure was always being carried. As Dora is dragging out dress after dress, I am giving her the too dressy, too sexy, too much boobs, comments, until I see a very pale lilac sun dress with a matching woven belt and spaghetti straps. I try it on and with my newly coiffed hair I am living my own little Cinderella story moment. I will go to the ball with Mr. Marcus charming.

The next two days I felt a little better and actually cooked a real dinner or two for the kids. I had asked around and found a sitter, but mostly I was counting down the hours until my first date after almost two decades of marriage. My date was Friday night downtown at a place called Spice. I naively agree to meet him at his apartment to park and then walk to the restaurant. I will come to realize that you never go to a person's home on a date, unless you really know the person well, but how did I know? I hadn't done this since I was 20.

I awkwardly navigate the organization of babysitter, kids' good byes, food for them, shower, hair, clothes and the ever-dreaded what shoes do you wear with this problem I drive downtown to his high rise which is fitting for an architect - all white modern, with a security guard perched in the lobby. I give him my name and next thing you know he tells me to head up to the apartment. My heart is pounding I still haven't been eating and it goes through my head to say a swift prayer that whatever happens, please don't let me pass out on this date. My mouth is dry I can see my chest pounding, accentuating how bony my collarbones look. The elevator opens and of course his door is straight ahead.

I knock, hearing the muffled music. I have no clue what to expect and before any more thoughts can highjack my brain, the door opens and he is tall. That's all I remember thinking, he is even taller and more handsome. He welcomes me and awkwardly tries to hug me, which I don't know how to react to. No man has laid a hand on me for a long time and I just freeze as the hug turns into an awkward "Hi, glad you made it! Was it hard to find?"

We are on the 23rd floor overlooking the city and the lake. He pours me a drink, which all of a sudden seems like both a great idea so my insides can stop shaking with nerves and an equally poor idea as I haven't eaten all day. We walk out to the balcony, and there is a very awkward moment where we are looking over the city beautiful and a cool breeze comes and he instinctively puts his arms around me and tells me that I can relax a little, I look gorgeous, and it's all ok. Which actually only serves to make me even more nervous and stumble on a heel as I blush and profusely apologize. He very charmingly and politely tells me again it's all ok. I try to compose myself as best a nervous haven't-dated-since-1992 blithering idiot can and mumble something about going to be late for our reservation.

We walk through the city weaving around the lake, through the kids and the homeless that flock to Orlando for warm weather nights like tonight. I am regretting the heels as we reach the restaurant, and the hostess seats us outside by the lake. We are now seated kitty cornered and he's staring at me, making my skin tingle in a both very uncomfortable and equally good way. He's looking at my face, my hair, my lips, studying me.

I start to feel like an art exhibit as he runs his gaze expertly over me. "Tiffany, there is something very unusual about you. I noticed it over coffee and again now. You have no idea how absolutely beautiful you are, do you? It's so refreshing, mostly you get to date women who are a 5, who act like they think they are a 10 and you are a 12 at least and yet are totally charmingly oblivious to it in every way."

He says it with such sincerity that my eyes immediately prickle with salty tears and shift my gaze over to the lake hoping he won't notice and that my tear ducts will drain before they spill drops over my cheeks. It's funny how some moments with certain people are frozen into your memory banks yet so many moments go forgotten. We spend the rest of dinner discussing children, art, history and the world at large, I eat a few pieces of the sashimi I ordered and mostly feel my attention locked onto Marcus and every word he says.

I study his face, the lines, his eyes that show depth of emotion, how he blinks too much when you ask him personal questions, how he laughs out loud and his face instantly becomes a little boyish. He's very easy to talk to and has a calm demeanor that is fascinating and enthralling to me. I have come to realize I like calm reserved men the most. Marcus asks for to-go boxes. I presume they are for him, but as we walk back to his apartment he hands them to a homeless man who sat on the steps of a church, and I am instantly in very serious like.

My car is parked at his building and I am aware that my baby sitter is $10 an hour that I don't really have. He asks me to go up to finish the wine and I agree, even though I am pretty sure that invitation has nothing to do with wine. I am filled with butterflies and nerves, I haven't been with anyone since my divorce and I don't know exactly what the dating etiquette is, which as my mind is buzzing with thoughts and theories, my body has been taken over with nothing but lust.

Marcus places his very large hands on my face and kisses me for the very first time softly, respectfully as if he is asking if it's ok, then more passionately until our mouths blur the lines between where he starts and I finish. Apparently we were not only instantly, mutually in like but deeply sexually attracted to one another also. Which answered a very pressing question I had from my divorce. Could you get your mojo back after such heartache and if so, could it ever be as good as before you lost it? The answer is a resounding YES!

I would say that a million profound thoughts were racing through my head, but the truth is I was for the first time in decades, doing what I wanted to do without over thinking everything to the point of inaction.

It was intoxicating, glorious and much needed escapism, I allowed him into my world, my soul. His eyes locked on mine intently, watching my face but saying nothing as silent tears escaped the corners of my eyes and dropped onto his bed. The tears of change, of emotion, of loneliness, and of hope that I would go on to love and lust again. I left his apartment feeling like I had left a large chunk of hopelessness there, in amongst the crinkled sheets and compassionate arms of a stranger.

Marcus and I begin to date and it is a frustrating mixture of no child-care, no time and what I at the time think is his extremely busy work schedule. I often wondered why he would possible want to date me. I am still seriously over-emotional. Probably half the time I see him ends with me in tears in his arms and he tries his best to keep me encouraged and positive, but mostly to no avail. He quickly becomes the only bright spot in my life, and I cling to him like a baby with a blanket just hoping somehow that would be enough to eventually fix my whole world, which of course was a foolish fantasy I held for those six months we dated. The weekends away, the nights together snuggling, the laughs, margaritas and deep meaningful discussions all amounted to not much as I misunderstood a very important fact about online dating. Unless you ask and confirm you may not be dating someone who is exclusively only dating you.

We were standing in his apartment, tears streaming down my face as he's eating chili from a bowl on his lunch break. I had caught him in a lie and this led to a Facebook search which led to an awkward conversation and me standing in his apartment like women scorned do, pleading for answers.

His answers were nothing I liked or related to. He told me that although he did love me, although he was seeing me "the most," whatever that meant, he too had been in a long marriage and wasn't ready to commit to dating just one woman. So, he was juggling a few of us and having no regrets about it, so much so that he also encouraged me to do it.

"Tiffany," he said, "you just got divorced. "You shouldn't be doing anything other than what I and most of the people on online dating sites are doing, which is dating multiple people and having fun. I never lied to you. You never asked. This is how it is nowadays. I will never run out of new available women to date and you will never run out of new available divorced men to date."

I stood there in disbelief, horror, and sadness as he finished his monologue along with his chili with these words, " Just remember, Tiffany, you are more beautiful, more attractive, more intelligent, more charismatic than 99% of all other women in any room. Pay attention, look around you, you will see." Tears blinded me as I ran from his apartment out to my car and drove home, sobbing to Jason Aldean. Seemed fitting. You may think I could never forgive Marcus but in a weird turn of events, I actually not only became friends with him, but actually even tried being like him.

3

Million Mistakes

The great thing about living in Florida is that you can visit the beach 365 days a year. My divorce had given me a whole new appreciation for its serenity, its beauty and its healing power. I had my children practically 24/7 and the entire putting on a happy face thing was not my forte.

On really bad days, I literally couldn't get out of bed but on semi bad days, my coping mechanism was to drop my children at school and drive the exactly 57 minutes to Fischer Park in Cocoa Beach, where I would sit on the beach for precisely three hours before heading back to pick them up. It was a total mental break from my house filled with unhealthy thoughts and memories, the debt collecting calls, the random people trying to help showing up at my door, and the claustrophobic anxiety that engulfed me every time I stepped within the four walls of my once marital home. Being at home was like maneuvering in a minefield of thoughts, memories and emotions. I could barely breathe and, at times, I literally passed out from stress that was invisibly holding me hostage in my own home.

I was a perceptual worrier, every decision, every conversation, every piece of new knowledge or information about my divorce swam constantly through my head. I blamed myself for the dismal outcome. I blamed myself for how everything played out. I was wracked with unjustness and self-blame and loathing. It was ironic that almost as soon as my divorce papers were finalized, I began to vividly see the million mistakes I had made. I began to see everything I had done as a reaction to the unknown. Every move I made, I had made from fear, from despair, from emotion. The more I sat on the beach the sun baking my skin to an olive brown, the more I could see clearly the very bad choices I had made from Day One.

Starting at the very beginning I would wonder how I could have been so ridiculous to ask for a divorce or separation with no plan, no end goal, and no ducks in a row. I have no clue what I was thinking, except that I needed to escape. I was, of course, aware that I hadn't worked out of the home for 12 years, but this never even once initially crossed my mind. I think I must have been walking around in a fog. Where in real life it was 12 years with no job experience, in my mind it felt like 12 weeks tops.

I think as a stay at home mother of three small children, I was working just as hard as I did in a paid job, so it never really felt like I just stopped working. The 12-hour shifts at Universal had been replaced by 24-hour shifts to various babies, toddlers, and preschoolers, all making demands of me 24/7. There were always, errands to run, cleaning to do, cooking, school runs doctors, and many extra activities. It just became a different kind of work.

What I failed to realize was it was a kind of work that you don't get credit for in the real world. For example, with HR recruiters and in competition to hundreds of other would-be employees, without such a huge "work gap." I had no plan, I was just going to get a job, get full custody of my children, juggle it all, and I was very much delusional in these thoughts.

I had started applying for jobs right away during my separation, and within weeks, I knew both from feedback and a giant reality kick in my bum that employment was very, very unlikely. I also had begun to realize just how much everything costs. If I were to get a minimum wage job, this plan also was totally undoable with three children and day care to pay for. I would sit on the beach and cry big fat tears of frustration and sorrow, falling behind my oversized sunglasses. I knew that I should have had a much better plan, a Plan B if my marriage hadn't worked. I hated yes hated allowing myself to become dependent financially on anyone. It felt dirty, almost as if I had lost my adult status and had reverted to a dependent child. I didn't want to be dependent on anyone, I wanted to show my children and myself that I could support myself, to feed them and clothe them.

I was blinded by a sense of just trusting that the court system and lawyers would somehow sort everything out and that I would somehow miraculously be ok. Even writing that seems ludicrous. I should have had a plan, a rock solid one, I should have retrained, reeducated, found a job while I was still married and before I even uttered the word divorce. I should have had that plan even if staying married was what I was going to do when all the kids moved out and I was an empty nester.

I ran my toes through the sand. The warmth never ceased to make me feel better. Oddly with the dramatic weight loss, also came a physical feeling of being perpetually cold. The beach at 98 degrees, with the sun directly blazing on my flesh and the sand red hot on my feet was as warm as I could ever get during this period. I could sit there all day alternating between a kind of relief I felt to be near the vastness of the sea, and sobbing waves of pain away as I watched the waves relentlessly pound on the shore line. The sea always made me realize just how small and probably insignificant I and my plethora of problems were, which in turn made them seem smaller even if only for a few hours.

I would spend hours there over-analyzing my life, both pre-and post-divorce. I had come to the conclusion that even during my marriage, I was probably far, far too trusting and passive. Maybe being a people pleaser, maybe being a middle child, I'm not sure what makes people one way or another, but in marriage I had somehow traded my last name in along with a whole lot of say in anything.

It was very clear that, we lived on his money, in his house, that I had no decision-making votes. Plus, I was kept so far in the dark that during the entire 16 years of my marriage, I had no access to any bank accounts, financial records, stocks or pensions. I had absolutely no idea how much money was made, or where or what it went towards. Self-employment is a divorcee's worst enemy and very much any spouse's ace in the hole. There are so many ways the person or lawyers can manipulate the figures, the assets, the worth, the losses, and the tax records. It is also well-documented in the family law arena as being a hard area to police.

I had no money when I divorced, no assets, nothing, I couldn't even find the initial $5,000 I needed as a retainer to file for divorce, and I had to open a credit card to pay for it. Thank God I had the foresight to even do this. Before and during my marriage, my credit score was very close to

800. It had been shocking to me and obviously yet another challenge to watch it plummet to 520 through my divorce. So many things I had taken for granted that I thought the legal system would address yet they did not.

The person who has all the money access knows you have no money. They psychologically understand they hold every single financial card in the game of divorce. They can get better lawyers, they can disclose only what they want to, and they can hide assets, stop working, and spend copious amounts of the supposedly joint money so you only get a portion of whatever is left. I have heard all these stories and more from our users.

As I have worked with so many divorcees through *Dreams Recycled,* self-employment leading to all these financial finagling is a common theme. As the waves crashed, I would ponder why I had accepted this kind of non-partnership in my marriage, I blamed myself for this. I went through this scenario in my head. What if before we married I had been clear that if I ever gave up my job I wanted full access and decision making on all finances? I didn't know how I would have had the whereabouts to negotiate this, but I took full responsibility for not. It's funny in a very unfunny way how when you are young and first married, having someone "take care" of all the finances seems quite lovely, but when you divorce "taking care" of them, it has a much more sinister meaning.

Another thing I struggled with was the fact that even though during our marriage my ex-husband made all the money, it was by law set out in the state of Florida 50% mine. Whether this was a mental brainwashing that had occurred during these years or the total lack of access and knowledge I had about finances, it certainly didn't seem in my head like my money. It really seemed like it was his and the divorce would be as our marriage was, all his way financially.

I very early on had accepted that I would never find a way to get money to hire a good enough lawyer and forensic accountant to really take control of the mess. I had, like a lot of people, not only struggled to find a way to pay them minimum fees but also struggled to find proper professionals to work on my behalf. Unfortunately, in divorce you often only get as much justice as you can afford.

Which brings me to another of the million mistakes; I should never have found a divorce lawyer using a Google search. I as a person with less than even limited tech knowledge had no idea how SEO (Search Engine Optimization) worked. SEO is a mostly paid for. Believe me, if you Google "best lawyer in whatever city," you will not actually get the best lawyer in most of the cases. Instead, you will, if you are lucky, get a good lawyer who understands the power of SEO and has spent the most money to show on the first page.

What I should have done is ask around, or check Avvo, for consumer lawyer ratings, or even ask other lawyers in other fields whom they would use for a divorce. I also didn't realize that you could interview a few of them to both see who you liked and also get a feel for who may work hardest for you on your case. I have to admit I was probably a bit of a conundrum for a divorce attorney - a grown woman with three children sitting in a divorce lawyer's office telling him that I had no clue how much money my ex makes, or what his assets were. Pretty extreme by a lot of people's standards. Then tell him that you have never seen any financial information in 16 years. They may as well have been dealing with a child.

For the most part, though, I would lay on the beach beating myself up about what I did wrong, and try to guesstimate what the outcome could have been. These constant, unyielding punishing thoughts I had did nothing to actually fix anything. It was just a list of a million mistakes and what-ifs that played in a constant loop in my head. What if I had found money for a trial? What if I hadn't settled in sheer exhaustion and despair? What if I had even known a figure for any parts of our asset? All the sun, sea, and sand were never going to change the outcome of the divorce or give me any real answers to any questions I may have had regarding facts and figures in my divorce. Mostly, I wished I had stayed financially independent.

What also bothered me a tremendous amount was that not once during my divorce did I think or consider that the Internet is full of information on divorce. I was so computer unsavvy and also so naive that I really just thought the court system and lawyers must know what they were doing. So I blindly went along with it. I didn't know my rights, I didn't know any divorce laws. I was in such emotional turmoil that I didn't think to research anything myself.

I had come to a very disturbing realization after the divorce was final that not only were there no real set in stone divorce calculations, (except child support) but that these meant nothing anyway when you had few or no facts and figures to go along with them. I also very quickly realized the courts are not set up to deal with one spouse having zero money assets and the other having full control over everything. I spent many of my beach hours wondering about divorce in the United States and thinking that the entire system and process is in serious need of an overhaul.

There also seemed to be no real lawyer intervention in my case. The lawyers had far less say, had far less advice than I would have thought they would, and my lawyers' answer to everything tended to be, "Well what do you think?" or "What do you want?" My response would always be, "Well don't you know the answer? This is a legal question!" In answer, they would say that there is no exact anything in divorce settlements; it's all negotiable. I had many hours laid there on the beach, acting out in my head a different scenario where someone would have guided me, given me basic information, helped me understand the entirety of it before I had even found a lawyer. I saw almost immediately that not being my own advocate and not being educated or guided by someone who knew what it was like had been very detrimental to my divorce and had also led me to believe that there must be a better way to navigate it.

I want to say those hours on the beach were wasted, relieving the horrors of divorce. I never really came up with a solid solution, but I did over time start to forgive myself for my many errors, flaws and mistakes I made during my divorce. I also was, in the process, learning to spend time alone. Alone was not a good place for me generally. It led to very dark thoughts and emotions. Sunning myself seemed to be a compromise between being alone and yet surrounded by people to watch and study and wonder about. I never spoke to anyone on the beach but just their presence made me feel a little less broken and removed from the world we live in.

Dating Marcus or anyone would definitely be shoved in the Million Mistakes Bucket. I was so not ready emotionally or mentally to have a relationship, I really believe no one is, directly after divorce. I thought I was mentally just so desperate to feel like I was both alive and had moved on that I jumped headfirst into a pool that was far too deep for this novice dater to swim in.

Everyone has their own way of coping and their own learning curve, but in hindsight, sitting on the shoreline, waves lapping my legs, I realized that I truly was undatable. Maybe not incapable of having fun dates with men, but certainly far from able to have a boyfriend that encompassed emotions and meaningful thoughts and commitment. I actually had really started to wonder how Marcus or anyone who was constantly hitting on me could be attracted to me. Didn't they see or sense how terribly emotionally annihilated I had been or was? Did they suffer from some type of saving syndrome? Or were they the vultures? Really hard to tell, but I knew even then on some subconscious level that I would never attract a healthy relationship while I had such an unhealthy one with myself.

The self-loathing, the depression, the feeling of worthlessness. This wasn't something any normal man should want in his life, so if I was going to get to that place I needed a massive amount of work on myself. Also lying flat on the sand, I was aware of how unhealthy my body was still. I knew that too needed to be fixed. I needed to take better care of myself, eat better, be kinder to myself, stop punishing myself for everything that not only had passed, but that I had no power to change.

The beach made these thoughts clearer. I didn't necessarily take action on any of them, but the fresh air and change of scenery definitely seemed to help align and organize them into little self-help lists for me to think about over the next few months.

Another dating home truth was that dating apps are addictive time wasters, you literally never run out of people, or possibilities, they fill you with 24/7 attention, attention I craved yet had no idea how to really deal with. I didn't know what I wanted from these men. It seemed at first that every "You are stunningly beautiful message" bought with it a kind of joy, a kind of validation that I really wasn't gross after all and maybe some man may once again love me. Yet every offer of sex, every man asking to hook up, every man sending photos or wanting photos, was also in equal parts eradicating any remnants of self-worth I had left. I had come to the conclusion that dating apps should be used sparingly and only for entertainment purposes directly after your divorce. The attention and interaction on them for the most part, I believe, does as much harm as good. For females, I think it's especially hard. You receive literally hundreds of messages a day; it's overwhelming, flattering, awkward and mostly shallow, all primarily based on looks, and the pursuit of sex. It's nice to be wanted but even I knew in this fragile state that it's only nice to be wanted for the right reasons.

I was ridiculously far from self-love at this point. I still felt a kind of self-imposed blame and doubt in myself for everything I had done and all decisions I had made. I hadn't been able to switch these thoughts off totally yet. I still I think was hoping for a miracle, a lotto win, a knight in shining armor, a twist of fate something that in an instant would right all of my life's wrongs. I would love to just blink like *I Dream of Jeannie* and have everything magically into place. I knew this was not going to happen though. I wish I had also known the time wasted on all these obsessive negative thoughts was time wasted that I could have been using to refocus on positive things. I guess the very first steps towards a positive life are by far the hardest to take.

If I was going to get out of bed, have no money, no job circumstances, being grateful for the gorgeous Florida coast line, being grateful that I could go to the beach during a school day, being grateful that my children where happy and fed and still had a roof, the tears and sorrow never changed or made anything better in any way. They never led to a pot of gold or a solution. It was a mistake to spend that time in that way. Maybe a little of it is necessary but 18 months of it probably a little much. I realized during beach time that I was, in fact, the poster child for screwing up my own divorce, for being uniformed, too passive and too naïve, I basically committed almost every mistake you could have. This feeling that I didn't want anyone else to do what I had with my million mistakes in a small way planted the seed of things that were to come in my life.

I really wanted a magical fairy tale to fix everything all at once, but that doesn't happen in real life. So I was left to drive home from the beach, with tan lines, a little more clarity and no real resolution. Just a slightly lighter heart and a healthy dose of vitamin D.

4

Simon Says

I don't have an awful lot of friends. There are many people I know and are friendly with but, for the most part, I am a very private person. My friends during my marriage were limited to mostly my Ex's friends and family, so I, like many other people, found myself very limited in the friend zone after my divorce. Which brings me to my first boyfriend, Simon.

You may be thinking that we dated at high school, but our relationship was confined to the years between seven and nine years old. He was my very first boyfriend and most likely the first boy who kissed me. This occurred in a very invigorating game of kiss chase at our local primary school.

I loved Simon, not just for his sparkling blue eyes and mop top 70s sandy hair, but also for his earnest pursuit of my affections even at seven years of age. He would cycle approximately three miles alone to my house to hand me love notes on little scraps of paper that he wrote in number two pencil with endearments such as "I love you." Quite the little determined Romeo, Simon was also fiercely brave, risking the protective unfriendly greeting by my father. Simon had the kind of stop at nothing driven streak that many people at 40 still haven't cultivated.

It was no surprise to me at all to find out that he had grown to become a very successful entrepreneur, dabbling in a multitude of businesses, from oil, mines and hospitality. If Simon was involved, you knew it would be a wonderful business. I know this because after losing contact with each other for many years, one of the very divorcee-like things I did was find him on Facebook and reconnect with him.

I was shocked when I found him. The last time I saw him had been filled with great sadness. His father had been transferred and they moved away from our small English country town. I vividly remember the look on his face as my mom drove to his home so we could say goodbye to them. Our moms chatting as moms do, while we just sat looking at each other in a weird stupor. When we reconnected, one of the first things Simon so eloquently said was that I was his first and in some ways deepest feeling of loss. We may have been young but when you lose someone you care about, especially through no fault of your own, the weight of the loss sits heavily in your heart and soul for years. Maybe even for a lifetime.

Simon is one of those people who combine brilliant intelligence with common sense and a very healthy dose of cutting dry wit. He was also my very instant new old best friend from the moment we reconnected. It was like days, not years and certainly not decades, had passed. He was living in Asia and had been for as long as I had been in the USA. He was a constant source of amusement in a very dark world. Over the first few months, I very slowly revealed to him the despair and desperately unhopeful situation I had found myself in. Which grew to become daily texts of support and weekly calls to check on me and to make sure, I think, partially that I was still alive.

Most calls consisted of me giving Simon a laundry list of grievances, unfair occurrences, tragic financial stories and tears. He would very patiently listen, console and try very whole-heartedly to give me solutions to things that actually had no solution. I couldn't change the outcome of my divorce, I couldn't get a job, and I most certainly couldn't sell my home, which had become a money pit of repairs. As with all the homes in Orlando in 2012, it had halved its value leaving it upside down at best.

During my darkest hours of my divorce, when I refused calls, never answered texts, cried until my eyes were both swollen shut and sore, I never once didn't answer or accept Simon's calls or texts. He always made me laugh even through the ridiculous amount of tears and did his best to encourage me and restore any remnants of my tattered soul and self-esteem that I had left. Simon, whether he wanted to be or not, had become a life jacket to me, keeping my head above water even when I very much felt like I would drown in my own sorrows and regular self-pity parties.

You may think my relationship with Marcus had somehow improved my life, made me more hopeful of things to come, or my own self-worth. But in actuality, Marcus had inadvertently managed to make me feel momentarily better, luring me into a sense of false triumph and forward motion before emotionally body slamming me back into the abyss of depression. Breaking up with him had just solidified to me my worthlessness, the feeling that I am not quite good enough to be his only girlfriend. This thought process had set me back frantically to my cocoon bed and to the one place I actually felt like I was semi ok.

Simon showing up in my life and being the sweetheart he is had saved me and given me a much-needed distraction from the misery. Chatting about old mutual friends, family, kids, his pride at being captain of our elementary football team, our mutual love for the number seven, how much better middle children like us are, ha-ha! Silly little chats that probably no one else except us would quite understand, we had reverted to seven-year olds and I for one was happy and elated to get to switch off with him here and there during the week.

By far, the very, very, very worst thing times a million about divorce for me was the feeling of having no control over anything financially. During my marriage, I had naively allowed my Ex, who is self-employed to handle all the finances. I had no access to any bank accounts, stocks or account retirement. I had absolutely no idea how much money he made, but I was well aware that it was his money. I was often reminded that he alone had earned it.

I had no concept of how hard it would be after my separation to return to the work force; I had a B.A. degree in History and three smallish children to look after. I couldn't go back to the hospitality field at Universal since childcare does not operate until 2-3 a.m., which was often when I used to return from work. My children had also been accustomed and thriving on me being a pretty damn good pre-divorce, stay at home mom.

I had the very unrealistic and non-practical idea that I would separate, get a job, still have my children full time and it would all just somehow fall into place. After all, I was aware that divorce statistics were high, but if other people could juggle it all and evidently find employment, why couldn't I? The financial part of the divorce journey had been crippling.

The worst days were when I had no money at all to buy food for my children, I wasn't going to ask for help, and the unpaid bills just kept piling up, with no reasonable solution to pay them anytime soon. Thank God for my children. They learned to ask for less or for nothing at all. They seemed ok eating cereal or two dollar mac and cheese for dinner, but it was emotionally devastated for me as their mother to have to explain, for example, why our car kept breaking down and we couldn't afford to repair it.

By far, the worst memory of financial hardship came in February of that year. My daughter, Tilly, loved being a ballerina. She was seven and what she lacked in skills, she made up for in sass. There may literally be nothing cuter than a little ballerina, from their sweaty bun heads to their pink tights and ballet slippers. She was signed up at the local ballet school, and had been dancing all year in her one leotard that I could afford from Target. I had somehow scraped together her $187 dance fee so we could attempt to do some semblance of normal with her routine.

Christmas came and the new ballet semester started again in February. I pulled out Tilly's pink leotard and tights and realized I hadn't replaced her ripped ones. My heart hurt as I immediately started to panic. *How can I buy her extra $18 tights?* I pull out her two pairs of dance shoes, her black ones for jazz and pink for ballet and I have that horrible sneaking suspicion that maybe they no longer fit. She seemed to have grown a foot in height just over the holidays, as kids do. I motioned to Tilly to get her dance shoes and she ran to me, as she basically only has one speed - "high." She plopped herself down on the filthy rug - our vacuum system had broken long ago and I certainly wasn't going to spend the little money we had on that.

"Mummy, they don't fit! I need new ones. The black ones are too too small, too, Mummy. Let's go now to the shops." I slumped to the ground next to her and began to sob. How had these $32 ballet slippers come to feel like a monumental amount? How had I been married to a man who by most people's standards had been very successful and yet I couldn't afford $32 to buy shoes for my daughter? And quite possibly worse, how did I become a 40 year-old woman with no skills and unable to support myself or my children? I don't know which of these thoughts was more depressing.

"Mummy, Mummy what's wrong? Its ok, do you have a headache again?" she innocently asks. I tell her though tears she may not be able to go to ballet this semester. Maybe she should take a break and go back the next one. She then proceeds to start crying with me. I become aware that Griffin, is watching us through the French windows and has heard our entire conversation. Griffin maybe a child of few words, but he has always been a child with a huge heart and abnormally high EQ. Without saying a word, he has gone to his wallet were his $50 from his January 13th birthday is kept. He takes it out, walks over to us and hands it to Tilly, saying, "Its ok, I will buy your ballet shoes, Tilly." This results in her smiling her huge smile and me disintegrating into more sobs. I try to tell him not to but it's too late. Tilly has his money and she does, in fact, go to ballet that semester in the shoes her 11-year old brother bought her.

I am recounting this tale to Simon. I can feel his discomfort on the phone from ten thousand miles away. He feels bad, and doesn't know what to say. He still doesn't understand exactly how I got to this place in my life and, quite frankly, neither do I. There is a lot of talk about laws, and lawyers and I reiterate with him that basically he who has the money in the family law system in Florida wins. That's it, really, plain and simple. I had long since quit explaining what had happened but I had in no way stopped whining about it.

On one such very whiny day, Simon made the mistake of calling me mid melt down, and I had a very long laundry list of problems for that day,

1. My lawyer sucked and kept advising me to just marry someone rich, as I was hot.
2. My AC was broken and it was approximately 98 degrees.
3. My car's power steering was gone.
4. My son needed $80 for a school field trip.
5. My Ex was still texting me.
6. My fingers kept going numb for no reason and I had no health insurance.
7. I hadn't been able to find even one job I was qualified for.
8. I had almost passed out at the circus in front of my parents who had tried to surprise us with the outing there.

And so on and so forth, somewhere during the list I could hear him huffing. I paused long enough in my tale of misery for him to forcefully and shockingly to me blurt the words, "Tiffany, for the love of God, I can't listen to this anymore, Get out of bed, go downstairs get off your arse, and make a list of every single thing in your life you can change. Instead of constantly telling me every time I call all the things you have no power to change, why don't you shift your focus to a list of what you can change!"

Me, being the Negative Nelly at this point in my life, began to indignantly respond with "Haven't you been listening to me at all? I can't change anything. I have no money. I have no job. I can't fix *any* of this."

"That is so totally not true, Tiff. You have a million more opportunities afforded to you than most people. Visit an orphanage, an AIDS treatment center, look up any third world country. You have a roof over your head currently. You have food. Don't tell me you are the worst-off person on this planet every time I talk to you!"

I immediately feel bad. My memory banks recall images of sick skinny babies with bloated bellies, trying to nurse from their malnourished mothers' breasts while flies swarm them, and I am immediately guilt ridden. So I just listen.

"Tiff, listen, you know I'm trying to help but this isn't helping. You need to focus on everything you can do. You can't change the outcome or the position you are in unless you start to realize what you can do instead of what you can't do. So, again, please go downstairs and make a list, a very simple list, of options and changes you can make, whether it's the grocery store you go to, or the places you run, or the way you dress, the way you do your hair or who you date. Whatever it is, just do it."

I, of course, have tears running down my face by this point, and even though one part of me was hurt by Simon's harsh words, I literally, in that one conversation, felt a shift, a giant reality kick in the arse that I had long needed. I had actually done very little to help myself except look for jobs I knew I wasn't going to get. I was so overwhelmed, I just didn't know how what or where to begin. I was waiting for one large answer, a kind of all-encompassing lifeline, a savior, a lotto win, but this was such an unrealistic plan or life goal.

Whether wittingly or unwittingly, Simon had in that one conversation changed the very biggest part of anyone's life - my attitude. I could feel my brain beginning to buzz with something I had long since lost sight of. Possibilities. It was late after our call. He had promised to check in with me to see what I had come up with on my list. I in turn was eager to show him that I could at least try to be more positive. I fell asleep that night with a new-found word on my mind - *change*. The following morning I awoke, and instead of the usual monumental effort it took to make it downstairs and through the morning with kids, I found myself hurriedly going from one chore to the next - dropping the kids off with a *I love you* and kiss, and almost happily racing home, not to go to bed, but to write my list, for Simon, for me, for my life to begin to change.

I still have my list, it reads as follows:

Things I have right now the power to change:

1. Hair.
2. Clothes.
3. Body.
4. Gym.
5. Church.
6. Books.
7. Friends.
8. Dates.
9. Food.
10. Kid activities.
11. Make up.
12. Knowledge.
13. Nail Color.
14. Furniture
15. How clean my house is.
16. How clean my car is.
17. Sleep.
18. TV/Movies I watch.
19. Saying NO.
20. What I drink.
21. Beaches I go to.
22. Music I listen to.
23. Things I say.
24. People I talk to.
25. Apps I download.
26. Bank.
27. Bedding.
28. Drawers/ Cupboards.
29. What I own.
30. Eyeliner
31. Thoughts.
32. Attitude.

My list wasn't earth shattering but they were all good, all doable if I wanted to. I took a deep breath and viewed my list over and over again. I may not have the power to change everything, I may not have the ability to do a lot of what I wished I could, but I did have power, in the form of choice, in the form of change. This was a *ginormous* improvement over my outlook on life up to this point. By nature, I had always been passive, from even a child, when I would hide behind my mother's legs when people tried to speak to me. To my marriage, where I had been railroaded into not having any say in anything except the children, really. I had just accepted what good, bad, or otherwise that had been bestowed upon me by fate, by others or by circumstances. Up to this point I was not even remotely aware that I had the power within to determine my own fate or destiny. Within 24 hours I somehow did. This was my first post-divorce upswing, given to me ironically my very first boyfriend (FBF).

5

Chunky Change

It took me approximately three days until I could really wrap my head around this new mystical land of change I had been transported into. It was similar to being lifted from a fog of *no* to a place with almost limitless yeses. I wandered around my house, which quite frankly I had totally let go in the tidiness department. It was filled with kids' toys, school project remnants, and clothes we had all outgrown, shrunk to not fit in, or just discarded as unwearable. I wondered what I could do to change it. It was almost exactly as the day my Ex had shown up with three very large moving men and taken whatever he wished to. Missing furniture, empty wall spots, but mostly it was still a weird, and I now very much see, an unhealthy shrine to our failed marriage.

The china cabinet held a dried bouquet, tiffany vases, Lennox crystal, and other unwanted wedding gifts. The more I started to notice, the more I saw what I had unknowingly been doing, and I was actually making my own divorce and misery worse. I was feeling sorry for myself. I was self-absorbed to the point that I was wallowing in it. I was listening to depressing music, I was reading depressing books, watching depressing movies, all while living in depressing surroundings.

So I borrowed $180 from my mother and ordered a dumpster. If I was going to change and my life was going to change, I was going to need to clear out my daily surroundings ASAP.

Dumpster Day arrived and I greeted the dumpster men with far too much enthusiasm. I am sure they thought I was certifiable, but my dumpster was going to be the first change I made. My garage was still stacked full, and I mean *full* of boxes from our move into that house ten years previously. It was also filled with a lot of junk, some of it was mine, some came from the kids. Some even came from folks who had long ago stashed something away. At this point it didn't matter. Possession was nine-tenths of the law and I put on my rubber gloves and started hauling item after item, box after box into the dumpster. It was summer, well over 80 and I was still ridiculously too thin, but somehow through probably pure adrenalin and joy, managed to go through almost every item from the garage and most of our wedding gifts. Most of those items took a quick trip to the dumpster.

It was so cathartic as I hurled plate after plate, books, papers, clothes, knick-knacks (what are knick- knacks? Anyway, I hate them). Not only were these items a waste of space, but with every item, went every memory associated with them. Every shared marriage memory got hurled, smashed, demolished, and removed from my house. A matrimonial purging of the bad, the anger, the sadness, the unfairness, the disgust lay smashed to smithereens on the bottom of a large blue metal dumpster. In that moment, I couldn't think of anywhere better for those divorce things to be.

Simon was proud of me for taking action. He too, I think, could feel a change in my attitude. Instead of crying, I was sending him photos of the stages of my cleaned-out garage. Not exciting, but better than the incessant whining.

While cleaning out my garage, I had been thinking a lot about what other changes I could make. And being in the garage and dumpster zone, I had become very aware that my only outside the house time ever was on the way between the car and school runs or grocery store. During this time, I wasn't doing much else. Since the Marcus disaster, I hadn't really felt up to the odd kidnappings by Dora and Nancy.

I stood by the dumpster and looked up at the sky, I was actually very fortune to live in Florida. Ok, so we have too many tourists and don't know how to dress for anything but 90-degree weather, but it most certainly is stunning weather. After updating my playlists to more upbeat music, I dug out some workout attire that I hadn't been wearing as PJS for the last three years, threw on some Nikes, and started running. Not a brilliant move as I was still barely eating. I was still, at times, feeling very close to passing out. And it was way too hot, but I did it anyway. The first day a mile, the second two miles. By a few weeks into my new found love I was running five miles a day and I was getting stronger. I was eating better, staying out of bed for longer periods, and even though I was having good, bad and other days, it seemed to relieve an awful lot of the stress I was still under. Some days I ran crying or in anger; other days I ran from loneliness; and some days I ran in happiness. It was the go-to activity of choice for me, and it also had kind of given me a routine to my day:

Kids' school drop off, run shower, either sleep again on bad days or try and be more productive on others, look for jobs, or clean house.

My life in no way had been fixed. I was still in massive debt, still had no plan, still had no goal. I began looking into various other job avenues, which made me happy, too, as I realized I really could "just" be whatever it was I might be interested in. I again scoped out some minimum wage jobs but after again calculating how much childcare would be I deemed them not even doable with three children.

Despite no progress at all in the job or financial areas of my life, I had very slowly begun to regain a very little, and I mean very little, amount of control over the depth of despair that each new obstacle brought my way. I started to ignore or not read texts from certain individuals that I knew only brought anger and sadness into my life.

I began to just not pay for things. Ok, well this is how this works. If you have a mountain of bills you can't pay, the old me would have stayed in bed and cried about the unfairness of the stack of bills I couldn't pay. The new me still freaked out when major things broke and we made do where possible. We lived without AC for about 10 months in Florida. We also figured a multitude of ways to do things as cheaply as possible.

I refocused all my energy on what I *could* do as opposed to what I couldn't do. I had made positive action as my daily mantra. It was a new religion for me, trying to make sure that each day I did something, just one thing under the umbrella of daily positive action, whether it was to list an item on eBay, put make up on, fix my hair, cook a healthy meal for my kids, or run five miles, just something productive and positive.

It is the single most important thing you can do when faced with any adversity. Take action, do not let it engulf you and drown you, but let it propel you to a place of doing something. Almost anything counts because the inactivity, the not moving forward, the lack of productivity will slowly and surely kill you, from depression, from anxiety, from grief from sorrow. No one should ever allow adversity in any kind to dominate and rule his or her entire being and mental state as I had. It's not necessary, not healthy, and totally fixable by taking daily positive action.

I actually threw Maxwell an entire birthday party for less than $25. I used box cake mixes and tube icing, I bought a big bag of popcorn, and popped it myself in our little machine, Seven dollars for ice cream and seven dollars on no name soda, and a red box movie. I recycled all leftover party plates from parties past and it was super fun! The kids didn't or could not tell that it was a $25 birthday party. Each little thing I accomplished became an *I can do* emotion within compared to an *I can't do* one. I was slowly but surely realizing there was very little I couldn't do when I focused and put my mind to something. Except find a job it seemed.

Looking for a job had become a strange kind of farce. I was going through the motions of looking realizing I have no skills for anything that actually made enough money for my kids and me to live on. I had to try to stay afloat by selling whatever I could on eBay – kids' clothes, household junk, anything I found. But it was hardly a job or an income, just a little boost to help out here and there. I had also been working harder to stay out of beds most days. I had actually found myself dressed after my run probably four out of seven days, which was a radical improvement in my depression level and overall state of mind. I had even begun to fit into some clothes again.

The thing about my kids during this time is that they really never appeared to see anything as radically different. Maybe they just accepted that we now had no AC, no fridge, no money for dinners out or large gifts. I was also working like mad to refinance my house in order to make the mortgage less of the monumental burden it had become. Houses around us were going into foreclosure left right and center. As much as I wanted to sell my house, I couldn't while it was upside down. I realized how fortunate we were in many ways to even still have a roof over our heads and even though it often felt like my house was conspiring to try to choke me into submission with never ending repairs, on good days I was grateful to still be there with my children.

Change was coming into all areas of my life. Not huge change but little subtle shifts here and there. Baby steps from what I thought, to how long I stayed out of bed, to whether I went to get a coffee with Dora and Nancy. I was definitely feeling more "normal," more present, and less of the perpetual victim I had been feeling for the last few years. So much more mental control because quite frankly the biggest change by far was not in day-to-day occurrences, but in the overall theory that I was fortunate in some ways compared to others and that I may not have to power to change everything but I most certainly had the power to change.

I had begun to revel in the small victories, the daily triumphs, the positive thoughts, the feeling that by the laws of nature, this too will all eventually pass. I had changed my attitude towards my life and, in turn, this had begun to gradually change my life. I even started acting like an actual divorcee and going out at night to nightclubs, getting dressed up wearing makeup and heels and leaving my house in the evening.

Dora and Nancy, in their never-ending guardianship of me, had started to insist I go out, not often but here and there. We danced, laughed, people-watched, and avoided the unwanted advances of the night club crowd who come out to play after dark. It was all an eye opener for someone who during her 16-year marriage, never went out. Initially it had been super awkward. I had no idea that men were so forward or touchy-feely in clubs. I had no idea that anyone would even be attracted to me or want to dance with me.

Dora had lent me appropriate going-out attire and also retaught me how to dance. It had been decades since I had done that, either. I was still in the bad mom dancing 80s. Luckily, I was a pretty fast learner. On one such night at a club, it was decided on my behalf that even though Marcus had hurt me and made me super (beyond) skeptical about dating that I should in fact start to date again. This time, like all other areas of my life where I had slowly begun to take control, I decided that dating would only be on my terms in my way.

I had decided that what I really didn't want or need in my currently scrambled mess of a life was an actual boyfriend, but that what I *did* want was to get out into the world and meet people, ask, questions, make friends and figure out the mystical creatures known as men. Marcus had shown me everything that sparkles wasn't gold and I, in turn, had had an epiphany that maybe in some ways Marcus' theory of dating multiple people was perhaps the better and more realistic way forward after all.

6

Diamonds Aren't a Girls' Best Anything

While in the never-ending brainstorming of how to pay my bills after my divorce, I had been acutely aware that really the only thing I had from my marriage of any value was my engagement ring. A beautiful 2.5ct round brilliant cut diamond that was appraised for $23,000. It was like an insurance policy. I believed that during your marriage and afterwards, if something catastrophic happened, you could just sell that bad boy for its value as I naively thought all diamonds held or increased in value. Why else had we been insuring it for full retail value for all the years we were married? I was about to find out I was extremely wrong.

On a particularly bad day I was having not being able to stand the heat from no AC, I swallowed my pride because let's face it, when walking into a jeweler or pawn shop, you are already on the wrong side of that transaction. You have already reached a place that you need the money and are the weaker one in any bartering system. They know you are a divorcee like me trying to pay your bills, or a relative of a deceased person trying to get a little something for an item of jewelry you would never wear. They also know the average person who walks into a jeweler is uneducated on the diamond they have and its real value. I had been avoiding the walk of shame into a jewelers for over 18 month. I had hoped it wouldn't come to this but that I would be able to find a job and keep my diamond to give to my daughter. The time had come, though, and in my head I had already preplanned the spending of the 23K value I was led to believe my diamond held.

I sat in my car in 90-degree weather. I had my three children in tow as I always, did. They were hot and disheveled, as all kids seem to stay in the summer in Florida. I held back tears and swallowed a lump in my throat as I viewed this day as a great failure to have arrived at the point that selling my diamond was all I could do. I again was met with that guilt of these poor kids having me as a mom when I can't even support them or myself. Also those annoying *how unfair it all was* feelings that came flooding back. I had bribed my kids to behave in the jewelry store with the incentive of sundaes from McDonalds on the way home. Three dollars was a small price to pay when I thought I would be leaving with 23K.

The jeweler I went to is in a nice area of town, and has constant, rather annoying, commercials on how they are the best place to buy diamonds or to sell them to their expert gemologists. I took my ring and my appraisal, what more could they want? We walked in and were greeted by a *how I can help you* from a female jeweler who quickly sized me and my children up and had no doubt determined that we were going to be time wasters since we probably could not afford anything in there. When I told her I had a diamond to sell, her face changed into the oh yes that makes more sense face and called over the diamond gemologist expert, who also sized us up.

There is something oddly humiliating, about standing in front of a stranger, trying to sell your only thing of value, something that had bound you in love to another person for decades and had produced three beautiful yet antsy children who were placing their small sweaty hands on the pristine glass cases looking at the sparkling diamonds and treasures below.

I placed the diamond ring on the counter. It shined brightly under the florescent lights. A beacon of hope, I thought, and a way out of some of the mountain of debt I had been left with. He picked it up, looking at it through the loop. "It's about 2.5 carats," he said. "Good clarity, slightly off in color, good cut. We can give you $6000 for it," he said smiling, like a cynical character from a Broadway show. As the kids fidget annoyingly, I explained to him that it's valued at 23k and he just shakes his head and explains that's only retail. Resale diamonds aren't that valuable.

I'm not sure if I'm being punk'd or he's serious or what is going on but I muster my strength to tell him that I won't be selling it there and motion to the kids to get in the car. I put on a happy face for them, tears stinging my eyes. Yet another lie I was told during my divorce. Could a diamond really lose over 75% of its value? The three ice creams began to seem like a huge outlay but a promise is promise and it was nice to see their little faces ecstatic about their treats on such a hot day.

My mind is racing I have a very random recollection of a Donny and Maria movie where she sells her hair to buy him a pocket watch chain and he sells his pocket watch to buy her a hair bow. This random thought sends me into floods of tears of unfairness again. I am trying to figure out if he low balled me because I'm English, or looked like I needed money, or is this normal or was he lying or were we sold a bad diamond originally? I am confused, angry, and again at a loss as what I will do to get out of debt.

Another thought flashes across my mind. How many other divorcees were getting ripped off, lied to and taken advantage of in their time of need, and in a not great emotional state? There was something very wrong with this that must have sat deeply in the subconscious of my brain for months to come. When I returned home, I decided to pull up resale values of diamonds on my computer and found some astonishing figures. Diamonds, when resold aftermarket to jewelers, usually only were worth 20-25% of their retail value. Pawn shops would statistically pay 10-20% of their retail value, I wondered if every bride and groom in the world would spend these ridiculous amounts on diamonds if they knew their true worth.

I returned home, defeated, and again was unsure of what, if anything, I could do next. I cooked chicken Alfredo and broccoli for the kids which had become their favorite post-divorce meal. I sat with them as we watched a movie and really wondered what on earth I could do to make money, or find a job. Later that night, I spoke to Simon and told him the horror story of the diamond. He, too, was flabbergasted and again offered his assurance that eventually something would give. Somehow it would get better, and I would find a job. I fell asleep praying like mad that he, in his infinite wisdom, was correct, because despite my more positive attitude and my daily positive actions I hadn't managed to really hatch a plan, or find any way to make money and this was getting desperate, and very mentally draining just not knowing what or how I was going to ever get myself out of the post-divorce vortex. I had, though, come to a definitive conclusion. The only person who was going to get me out of it was me.

7

400 First Dates

Dora and Nancy had hijacked me from my house for another dating advice session. I had now navigated away from Match.com and onto a bunch of free dating apps that, well, let's just say had a mixed bag of users. Plenty of fish. You could place a profile on for free and exchange messages with no cost, which was a better idea for me under the current situation. They also have a ridiculous number of users who no doubt copy and paste to many women as they are playing the numbers game. My first day on POF, I received 400-plus messages. It was flattering, exciting and a little scary when you opened some of them to graphic descriptions of what they would like to do to you sexually. The keyboard really makes lions out of mice. I very much realized that no one would probably have the nerve to say what they were saying if it wasn't from the safety of an anonymous user name and miles of distance.

"I can't believe it babe, how can there be so many weirdoes out there," Dora said. I had no idea, either, I responded. I'm still fixated on where are the five orifices that one guy wants to stick his tongue in. We start laughing, Nancy tries to get me to answer the messages of all the really manly looking macho men, but instead I gravitate to the more reserved-looking professional ones who seem like because their necks aren't wider than their heads, that they may have jobs and not spend their life pumping iron and counting protein grams.

I am, however, won over by some of the more witty or fun messages, and reply to these men, too. For the most part, the men I answer fall into two categories the "man with a plan" or the "perpetual pen pal." Some men right away wanted to nail down a time, place, and date to meet, while others, wanted to know how many siblings I had, what my favorite color is and what I like, before even suggesting a real in life meeting.

It was fun to read the messages, drink wine, and giggle with my BFFS. They never ran out of witty comments, or good observations. Dora was like a Russian ice-skating judge. She viewed them all critically and made snap decisions on whether they were worth going on a date with or not. "No, No, no no no! Next, no-yes-maybe. Show me another photo. How tall is he? No, too short, too much forehead, too old, looks dopey, does he have teeth?" And on it went, scrolling through thousands of potential dates.

Nancy, on the other hand, was much less critical, saying most of them would be ok-ish, although she wasn't sure I wanted to date so much older than me so, on her urging, we lowered the ages in search to the same as me. If nothing else, it was amusing, reading both the messages and the men's profiles. I couldn't help but notice that some men suffered from kind of reverse anorexia. They clearly looked in the mirror and saw a super model where really they were more akin to Attila the Hun. Then to read their profiles, with the ridiculous laundry lists of demands:

Must be fit, must be stunning, must be a size 2 or smaller, must be financially secure and not expect me to buy dinner, and on and on. It struck me that men really do have it made in the lack of insecurity department, I know many stunning women, who rarely feel pretty enough or good enough and yet men from all races, sizes, social economic backgrounds and education levels have no problem telling anyone who will listen that they are the bees' knees.

"Have you heard from Marcus?" Nancy asked. I was apparently just reaching the part where I could talk about him without getting upset.

"Yes," I said. "We spoke but I'm not seeing him anymore."

"Great 'cause why would you? You have a million more men to go out with now?" Dora chimed in.

"No, it's not because of that; it's because I think as much as I hate what he was did to me, he is right. I shouldn't be dating to have a serious relationship. I have never been single my entire life. I went from a high boyfriend to my ex fiancé and then husband. I don't really know what I want or whom I want. The more I think about it, the more being an adult, getting dressed up, being treated well, getting out of my house, and making new friends seems like a much better option right now."

"Wow that's really grown up of you. Is this the real Tiffany?" Nancy teased, "But yeah, we can live through your dating life and now at least you won't be such a disappointment to us as a single hot woman. Get out there, have fun, smile, laugh and be happy, Tiffany! Look at all these men who want to go out with you! Let someone be nice to you and treat you well."

"It's what you deserve and it's time," says Dora.

I agree I said, "Let's be an adult and date for fun." I couldn't even believe these words were coming out of me. I'm much more an introvert at heart, meeting a plethora of new people is always daunting for me. One-on-one, I'm a little better but I was seriously banking on the man having the persona to carry the conversation and make me feel relaxed. Parts of me were still battered and bruised and I wasn't so sure I was lovable or even likable or that interesting as I often didn't have a lot going on in my life. Well, I certainly wasn't going to share any real life stuff on a first date with anyone, not even Dr Phil.

Within a week I had dates schedule for every free night of the week. I had and a couple of lunch and coffee dates dotted in between when the kids where at school. I had my calendar pretty much filled. Dating was going to be my new hobby and, like everything else I do in life, I did it with a passion.

Dora had yet again kindly lent me clothes. We had also arranged for me to meet some of the men in a coffee house near me where Dora and Nancy could spy on us while they were having coffee, too. After all, what are besties for? Night dates I was on my own, but the girls had made me pass along names of all the various men I was meeting and locations of dates. I was then to check in to make sure I hadn't been kidnapped, which I guess you can't really be too careful about these days.

One of my first dates was with a very nice man named Rob. He was an executive at a university, and was kind, articulate, and smart. We had a nice dinner and he made sure to put me at ease. He asked most of the questions. I answered. He asked me what I like to do, and I replied that I like to go to the beach with Tilly and that I like to take the boys to movies.

After giving Rob the dissertation on what I like, he very politely said " Tiffany, you didn't tell me anything *you* like to do, only what you kids like to do. " He again asked, "What does Tiffany like to do?" and in that one defining moment, he instantly knew and verbalized that I was not dateable yet and I knew on a very deep level that he was 100% correct.

I didn't know myself. I had just become someone's wife, room mom, mother, and daughter-in-law. I had totally lost all knowledge of what and who Tiffany was - her likes, her dislikes, and even though I was still at the very start of my journey to enlightenment, I had begun to understand the theory that if you don't know yourself and haven't found your way in the world, how could anyone else of any real value want you in their life too?

My date with Rob turned out to be another important part to my story. He was much more self-aware and knowledgeable of human nature and of divorce than I was. He, too, had been married to a stay-at-home mom, and had witnessed firsthand the lack of jobs out there for returners to the work force. The date turned very quickly from romantic into more life coaching. He strongly advised me to find a Plan B asap because if I didn't, not only would I run totally out of money, I would still be unemployed and only another year older.

He also very wisely informed me that most men who date after divorce are not looking for another dependent but an equal, and if I wanted to be viewed as one, I needed to somehow find employment anyway I could as soon as I could. I listened intently. He seemed to certainly know what he was talking about. It was eye opening to just get to speak with another divorcee and hear logical, smart, practical advice on what is a better way to move forward.

One of the strange things about my divorce is that I never ever spoke to anyone who was divorced. I actually, shockingly I actually, shockingly, didn't know anyone in my small circle of friends who was divorced. I never went to counseling, or joined a group for divorce adjustment. I never asked anyone for help and I most certainly had no practical advice on it up until this date. The words that ran though my head while he said each valuable sentence were, *I wish someone had told me this earlier. I wish I had known. Why isn't this out there? Why don't we know this?*

Seemed crazy that there was such a lack of practical advice out there for divorcees and, more importantly, in that moment for me. I left that date with actually more fear that I had better somehow come up with a master plan for my future. The pressure was immense. It really was each day turned into another day and a week with no resolution. Or worse, no plan.

My dates continued. For the most part the men were gracious, polite, decent men. But under the belief that truth is always stranger than fiction, I had my fair share of let's call them interesting ones. I went on dates with sons of celebrities, with professional athletes (or claimed to be), musicians, nerds, CEOs, CFOs, lawyers, doctors, salesmen, executives, magicians, hypnotists, models, chefs, professors, teachers, entrepreneurs, realtors, investors, stuntmen, art collectors, hospitality employees, men in the military, entomologists, gemologists, a bunch of other ologists, fashion designers, sadly no butchers, bakers, or candlestick makers for the full set of date cards.

It was a year of saying yes to anything, (well almost anything). As long as the man didn't seem like a serial killer, didn't seem like a stalker (those misjudged here and there). Mostly, though, I picked men whom I thought would be interesting and able to hold a conversation. The men were fascinating on all levels as I went from one date to another, I became acutely aware of really how little contact I had had with men since my marriage. I had no male friends. I was a stay at home mom, so I had no male work colleagues. Really, in hindsight, I had lived a ridiculously confined lifestyle.

I really had thrown myself into motherhood with 100% of my being and the only males in my life had been my two sons. I studied these dates intently, the brand of their shirt, how manicured or calloused their hands were, the way they looked at me, the way they read the menu, what they ordered for dinner and what they drank.

My dates became my own personal self-growth experiment. Of course, I secretly hoped that amongst them might be the one that man who gave me butterflies and whom I couldn't live without, but that never happened. So instead I observed, and I listened, intently to every word they said, read between every line and I'm not going to lie, built a pretty clear picture of the person I believed them to be all in the 45 minutes of our coffee date or the three hour dinner.

I probably won't know if I am right or not, but I saw narcissistic tendencies, passive aggression, residual anger from their exes, arrogance, neediness, insecurity about their looks, their success, or their intelligence. In equal parts, I saw and recognized kindness, humility, brilliance, wit, sarcasm (my favorite) confidence, security, passion, and decency. These good men, I doubt, realized at the time they were slowly repairing my thoughts on mankind. Any kind of compliment, or kindness shown, someone asking if I was cold, did I need anything, telling me I was beautiful, smart, sweet whatever it was that showed any kind of human decency, I reveled in and absorbed it like a sponge starved of water for decades.

Quite a few of these men made me cry on dates, not from anger or sadness, but from kindness. I don't think people realize how devastating divorce can be to the human condition. You have no one show you kindness or concern for so long. For all those men who met with me and made my year a little more bearable and who taught me that the world could be kind, I still thank them in my mind today. Men who have probably long forgotten me, I still remember. Not all of them, though some I remember in odd fascination, like date #4, I haven't really been on 400 actual dates but there were a lot, maybe 100 or so. But 400 seemed to be the perfect number of exaggeration that it started to feel like, and Dora and Nancy deemed must be it must be 400 by now.

So many more dates occurred with not as dramatic outcomes. But all interesting nonetheless, so I dotted them throughout the rest of the book, for your amusement.

Date #4, under the idea that truth is always stranger than fiction

I had connected with a charismatic, seemingly dynamic CFO, of a pretty large company. We texted back and forward for a few days, and he seemed nice, charming, smart and successful. All good. We arranged to meet for lunch, our first date, my moniker on my online dating profiles was butterfly, a symbol to me of finally coming out from my cocoon bed and trying to once again enjoy life.

He greeted me at the door to the restaurant, nice smile, well dressed, and escorted me back to booth where he had been waiting. In the booth was a Styrofoam cooler, which he gestured for me to sit next to it because it was a gift for me. I awkwardly sat next to the box, the thought transplant organ went through my mind and I looked around trying to scope out the nearest exit. I sat and he reached over, placing the quite light but too large for the booth cooler box on my lap. We are in a room full of people, I see the lady next to us eyeing the box with interest as he urges me to open. "Took me all morning to get that for you, had to drive to the other side of town." I started to lift off the top of the box, "Careful," he says. "Be slow."

Now I really am starting to get a little worried. Bomb, animal, body part flash through my mind. Upon opening the cooler top, I see a lavender mesh box, a very pretty one, with a big bow and a card on top. He instructs me to read the card. *To my beautiful butterfly, here's to the start of our new life together.*

Mmmmm is that sweet, I wonder, or odd, or desperate, or just optimistic. It can be taken so many ways. Take the box out, he urges, excitedly. I thank him for the card I don't really know what else to do. As I lift out the lavender box from the cooler, I see its packed in dry ice, I also see the box is entirely filled to the top with what at first glance looks like tissue paper of multiple colors. I go to take the lid of this mysterious box, and he again instructs me to be very careful with it. "Just peek."

So I do and what at first glance seems like stacked colored tissue paper is in fact tissue paper layers with the beautiful stunning actual wings of hundreds and hundreds of what I at first think are dead admiral butterflies, but what he assures me are only anesthetized ones that will wake up and fly when I take them home and thaw them out from the dry ice. Well, that wasn't quite what I expected. He goes on to explain to me that there is a superstition that if you whisper a wish to a butterfly, it will carry it up to heaven for you and your wish will come true. That part in it self seemed quite lovely. I was, though, still flummoxed by the over-the-top kind of bizarre gift I was given.

We looked at the menus and ordered. The conversation went back to being somewhat normal - "What do you like to do?" "Who watches your children?" "What's your schedule?" This all seemed pretty standard first date questioning. That was until he declared I was indeed the one as he had expected and that we should sync our calendars for the months ahead. "Do you ski?" he asked, "We will be going to Vail in March. " It was January. "We have a wedding to go to in Boston, in June and, of course I will want you to travel with me on my business trips as much as possible."

This all would have, like the butterflies, sounded and been quite lovely IF I was in a serious relationship with this man. Or if I even knew him. But I had just met him not 20 minutes before. I mumbled kind of random comments that matched his statements mostly because I really didn't know what else to do. "Yes Boston is lovely, no I don't ski, how lucky are you get to travel so much." We continued through lunch and already I was dreading the goodbye. What do I say? What will he say? What the frick do I do with 600 anesthetized butterflies? Do they really make wishes come true because right now I was tempted to wake one of their little sleeping winged creatures up, whisper in his ear "save me and hurry," and throw him up to the heavens in the hope that I would escape this strangeness instantaneously.

Lunch ended and as we left the restaurant and he tried gentlemanly to carry the butterfly box to the car for me he said very casually, "Oh, I have another gift for you in it in my car." My face and mouth froze. I mumbled that I was late for appointment and had to leave and that really 600 butterflies was way more than enough of a gift. I jumped into my car, quick as can be, and as I drove away I heard him say, "Its ok. I will give it to you next time."

As I drive to my children's school, I am confused by the lunch date. At this point, I had still only been on maybe four dates. Was this normal? Maybe he was just very into me, my ego said. Maybe that's how men who know what they want act these days. As I sit in my car in the car line, waiting for my kids to race out of school, my text sound startles me out of the deep thoughts I was having. I look down and see its him. I open the text and it's not a message but a photo. I look at it for a few seconds. I am not familiar with what it is. Looks like a metal shower curtain rod with two black rings one attached to each side, I reply with a simple question mark. Almost immediately he responds with two words. "Leg spreaders."

The good thing is that *leg spreaders* is pretty self-explanatory even without an S&M knowledge. Just at that moment my kids jumped into the car in their usual too chatty too energetic way. I closed out the texts before they saw and drove home, still bewildered, a little scared, and also curious about this very strange last few hours of my life with this undoubtedly bizarre, yet interesting man. That evening after school was normal, with the kids, homework, dinner, showers all being a blur of activity until bedtime came. I took a shower, crawled in bed and not until then did I read his following texts.

I haven't been completely honest with you it read please text tonight I want to speak with you.

The children had been fascinated by the butterflies and I had found all the instructions for how to release them into the skies. They were still in the box for the release day the following night when we had more time to do it. I did want to thank him. As weird as it was, it was still a kind gesture. But now I couldn't help but wonder what he wasn't honest about. "

"Hi." I texted

Hello, I was worried I wouldn't hear from you.

"No its ok. I wanted to thank you for the butterflies. Definitely a unique gift. Kids are thrilled with them."

You are welcome.

"Well before you say what you want to say, I looked up what leg spreaders are and I am totally not the girl for you."

Yes you are you are exactly the girl for me and that's what I wanted to talk to you about. It can be intimidating but I can train you and I think you will grow to like it. But the truth is, I don't want to date you. I want to own you.

Now for a pretty inexperienced female in the sex world, I am again unsure of what he is talking about, but me being me, I now want to know.

"What exactly do you mean? I'm not familiar with this."

What's your email, Tiffany? I am sending you something,

I oblige. It's also way before I realize that giving out your email to strangers is not a brilliant idea. A few minutes pass and I check my email and it's an attachment labeled *Contract.* I open it and begin to read its 21 pages. The first page lays out the terms, with two blank lines for two people's names. *I _______________, now known as slave, give myself to _______________, now known as Master.* From there it digresses into page after page of sex options, toys, role play, food play, things I never even knew people did or thought were even sexual. It was fascinating, bizarre, and partially sinister as it set out one-by-one the obligations of the slave to the Master.

The first 18 pages all focused on what the slave was expected to do for the master. The last three pages focused on what, in return, the Master does for his slave. The slave, was to get two weekends a month off, all travel and hotel expenses paid worldwide. The slave was to have all her sex toys and sex clothing, paid for. She would also receive an allowance per month for personal upkeep, nails, hair, gym, tanning, etc. I could hear him texting in the background but I was too busy being sucked into the contract. Do people really do this? Is this a joke? I answered his texts and explained again that it wasn't my deal at all; I also forwarded the sex contract to Dora and Nancy with a giant *OMG!* As friends do.

My would-be Master had a hard time accepting no as an answer, but eventually he got the message and disappeared. But Nancy, Dora and I spent many conversations discussing pages 1-21. We had to Google half of it. I think they both were surprised at how an innocent online match lunch date could end with a sex contract. I was later reminded that in some ways that contract may be the best offer you can get from a man as it legally laid down exactly in black and white what was expected of you and what you would get in return.

8

Dream Believer

My job hunting was still at a standstill. One day a week I would scan for new ads, try and send begging emails with a half assed resume attached to companies that I prayed might at least interview me, but to no avail. I was still drowning in debt, and I still had no light at the end of any tunnel, and worst of all, I think in hindsight, I wasn't even working towards anything. To have no direction, no clue, no plan, no goals is its own kind of purgatory. You are waiting for something but you actually have no idea what. A sign, a break, a miracle or perhaps even a dream.

The stress of divorce and of not being able to support yourself or pay your bills wreaks havoc on your sleeping patterns. Since my divorce, I had either not slept at all or slept for three days straight. Or I slept and had almighty nightmares and stress dreams that actually made me not want to sleep at all. Since my Simon-induced attitude adjustment and a more productive day, I still hadn't got back into a regular sleeping pattern. On March the first I had received a slew of unpaid bill notices, and I was still unable to control the rush of negative emotions that flared up every time I opened one and felt the stabbing of an unjust system. I fell to bed that night with must anxiety and stress. During the night I felt aware that I was dreaming something negative and stressful. I tossed and turned, I guess, trying to wake myself up from the very long dream that held me in its grasp for most of the night.

I was in a courtyard. It wasn't very wide and rows and rows of small shops lined up next to each other. Each one was a jeweler, some white shops, some pastel shades, all with different signage in the windows, "We buy gold," "Sell us your diamond." I was holding my ring in my hand and the three children were smaller but still mine in tow. I walked into the first shop and showed the jeweler my ring hopefully thinking he would give me the 28,000 dollars. He took a glance at it and said, "I will give you a dollar."

I started to say something but I just leave. He must be joking, I think. I grab the kids and walk into the next shop. "How much will you give me for my ring?" I ask.

"Two dollars, that's the best I can do," he's says. I'm starting to get upset in my dream. I take my kids again, shop after shop, up and down the rows of jewelers. Each shopkeeper offers me a dollar or two. After the 6 or 7th shop, I start to plead with the jewelers, "You don't understand! I have to feed my children. The ring is worth $28.000. You can't give me a dollar for it!" I try reasoning with them, but they still all say the same thing. My children are getting cranky in the dream. I'm at my wits end, on the verge of screaming at them to please help me, when all of a sudden, in my dream I say, "Screw this! I am going to sell my ring and everyone else's rings on a website called *Dreams Recycled*. I'm not going to let these jewelers rip me off, or anyone else off."

I awaken, and I not uncharacteristically remember my very vivid dream. I have always since a child remembered them in graphic detail. What is uncharacteristic was that when I woke up I thought, *Wow! That's a great idea! Someone must be doing that already. So much divorce in the world, someone must have a website for it.*

I took the children to school, and the dream was stuck in my head. Where did people's divorce items go? What did people do with this stuff? Smashing it into a giant metal dumpster and selling your ring for 20% of its value really didn't make logical sense. On returning from my school run, I opened the laptop my sister and parents had bought me for my birthday. I searched *sell divorce rings, sell rings,* and *sell unwanted divorce items,* page after page of nothing. All I kept finding were dismal divorce site forums of negativity and doom and gloom. I also found plenty of divorce lawyer aggregators, not one single place, though, dedicated to selling divorce items, dresses, and rings. So then I thought, *Well maybe divorce isn't that common after all*. Remember, none of my close friends were divorced.

I began reading and absorbing information like I was Bradley Cooper from *Limitless*. Not only was it all fascinating, but it was also horrifying. How can there be 1. 2 million divorces a year in the USA alone, one every 13 seconds, yet NO really good website to search for anything divorce related. Was I the only one who thought this was odd? Wedding websites, I knew off the top of my head, there were a few great ones, *The Knot, Wedding Wire,* but divorce ones, I couldn't think or find any for divorcees. No wonder I had been lost and made so many mistakes in my own divorce. I had a recollection of briefly looking for a place to go online and giving up. Now I saw why.

I spent the entire school day, reading divorce stats, government reports, discovering that divorce is a 50 billion dollar a year industry. That 43% of divorced women live at or below the poverty line after divorce. As dismal as that figure is, it made me feel better. I thought it was just me. I thought I was probably the only loser divorced woman who couldn't sort her life out and get a job after her divorce. The more I read, the more not depressed I became, and the more indignant that there were so many of us out there with nowhere to go and nowhere to sell your rings etc. for a fair price in a less humiliating way than getting taken advantage of by a jeweler in your darkest hour.

I started making notes. At the time, I had no idea what for but I did. I also searched for *dreamsrecycled.com*. I thought maybe subconsciously I had seen it somewhere before, but low and behold it came up under a website called *Godaddy* for $9.99. I even bought the domain name. I wasn't sure why and I felt guilty about spending that money on a whim but it was such a specific dream, I felt it was supposed to be mine or in a way already was.

My kids again came home from school and I was still distracted as we went through the nightly routine. Why wasn't the divorce community really being catered to? I couldn't wait to put my kids to bed because I knew the one person I needed to speak to, the only person I actually knew in business who I thought would tell me the truth about whether this could actually be a business idea.

Simon had no tech or website knowledge but he was the smartest business person I knew. With a 12 hour time difference, nights were morning for him and mornings where nights for me. I called him bright and early and probably woke him, yet he didn't care really as I retold my dream to him. I then read him the facts and stats and figures. I was waiting for his reaction because I figured worst case he would say it was stupid and I could just put it down to a brief momentary mad thought, probably not my first or last as I was known for thinking a little outside of the box.

"Tiff I think that's actually a really good idea, I think you can get a pretty decent website pretty cheap, why don't you look into it," he cheerfully said. I could tell from Simon's voice that not only did he genuinely think it was a pretty great idea, but that he was proud of me for having it and for getting to a place of even being able to think about this crazy idea that no one had done. Simon was traveling the entire next week, so bolstered by his stamp of approval, I started asking other people, friends, and family what they thought. My dad instantly and definitely said it was a brilliant idea. My dad is a successful musician and business man who always supported us all and recycled his life and career successfully and impressively multiple times.

"You should do it," he said. So now I was two for two for men who I looked up to in my life. Then I asked my mom, whose approval isn't as hard to get, being the perpetual cheerleader and supporter to all three of her children. We apparently are all geniuses and brilliant at everything. She also liked it. Then on my brother and sister who are actually in real life both closer to the genius zone than me. My sister is a very smart, dedicated and compassionate ER physician, who responded, "Yes, great idea! Then you can sell it and support us all when I sell it off," she teased. My brother is a little like Simon. A multitalented designer and entrepreneur who also tends to think outside of the box and succeed at whatever he's interested at the time. He also gave it a business idea thumbs up.

I spent the next 48 hours again searching the Internet for other divorce stats, figures websites etc. Could this really work? Could a girl from another continent, with no skills, who's unemployable, really start her own business? Could I make it successful and could I make money?. What was becoming clear was that what I was lacking in skills I was feeling in passion. I was leaning towards trying to make a go of this even though I knew nothing about the Internet industry. But what I *did* know was that I could do it from home, on my laptop that I already had. I had searched the average costs of website etc. and figured that maybe a $3,000 gamble to have a money making business was worth it. Three thousand dollars. I couldn't live on that for long, and I wasn't aware of any other bricks and mortar or franchise or even work from home business you could start for less than 20K. More like hundreds of thousands of dollars that I didn't have. I had looked at opening a boutique, a temp agency, and many other businesses. Really, pretty much if you could think of it, I looked into it. Which was making the job search even more frustrating, as people would offer their best suggestions and I would glumly say. Tried that, too expensive, and on and on.

One of my best friends, a fellow mom of Maxwell's friends, who had also unfortunately heard a lot of my divorce drama, is married to a corporate lawyer of quite a large firm. I told her my idea, which she too thought, was great and I also asked her if her husband would help me figure out what and how to start a company. This part I knew from searching about how to start a company and from the multiple companies my Ex started while we were married. I needed to be an official company. What would my company be called? And, by the way, how was I going to have my own company? It was exhilarating and terrifying, but it would be mine. Something no one, I hoped, could take from me.

As I mentioned much earlier, all my life I have loved the number 7. So with that thought and after bouncing few ideas off kids, people, anyone who would listen really, my friend's husband began the paperwork to incorporate my new and sole proprietor company. Heptagon Concepts LLC. Lucky 7 or so I hoped. Doing business as DreamsRecycled.com, I really couldn't ask for better friends and family during my divorce, I have to say anyone fake, false and non-supportive had basically culled themselves from my life during my divorce. People who had ulterior motives had also vanished, and the few awesome friends I had were as helpful and supportive as an army of 1000. Anita, Lois, Kim, Melissa, Jennifer, Leonda, even my UK friends who are more like family really, Anne, Theresa, Julian and Tim, encouraged and supported me in so many, many ways. I am forever indebted to them. Even Marcus, had become a friend and was eager to help and support.

I had already told, of course, Nancy and Dora who unfortunately knew exactly how much financial quicksand I was in, and they were supportive and happy. But also, I think, more worried than the rest of my friends about my throwing money I didn't really have into a business I knew nothing about. They were very helpful, and did what they could to be supportive.

March 13, 2013, was by far one of the best days of my life. Kim's husband sent me the official paperwork. I was no longer unemployed, although probably still unemployable. But I did not care because I was now not just a non-skilled single divorced mother of three small children. I was also CEO, of my very own company. I can't even begin to explain how ecstatic this made me. I phoned everyone I knew, joyfully screaming down the phone. My friends screamed back because that's what friends do. It was determined that this called for girls' night celebration. The weight of the *no plan-no goal-no clue* had been lifted. I had a focus, a goal, something to take action towards. Even better I had somehow found the confidence and belief in myself, something I had for decades struggled with to take a miraculous fortuitous dream and turn it into a realty.

Whether win, lose, or draw, I was sticking by my decision to take this humongous leap of faith in my idea, and myself and this leap alone instantly propelled me 4,000 miles farther in my own divorce-healing journey. I wouldn't be the victim of my divorce or my circumstances, I wouldn't idly sit by and wait for someone or some man to save me or give me anything, I was going to take the one life I had been given and do something that not only I believed would help me and support my family, but also would support many other divorcees in their journeys.

Daily positive action over the previous eight or so months had bought me to a place where I really believed I had a shot at making it work. I could take this opportunity, this idea and really give it a go, throw all my energy, productivity, creativity and enthusiasm into it. What did I have to lose? So that is exactly what I did and I did it with a ferocious passion.

Date #112
Who Doesn't Like Hot Men?

I generally don't go for model looking men, but he had been very nice on a dating app, so I agreed to meet him for coffee while the kids where at school. On first impressions, he was well, kind of wow. We ordered coffees and sat at the stools they sometimes have in Starbucks. He was a divorced dad, former model, and currently some kind of business owner. I watched him as he ran his eyes over my body. He then asked me how often I worked out. "Oh I don't know," I said, "a few times a week. How often do you work out?"

The former marine then decided to give me a blow-by-blow account of every move and hour spent, five days a week in the gym. He acted out the moves where he could. For 20 minutes straight, he described his work outs, finishing up by lifting his shirt up and showing me his killer six pack, before declaring he has 1% body fat and he's all muscle.

I tried to make an excuse to leave, and said it was getting late. He replied that he lived really close and actually I didn't have to get kids for 30 minutes, which was just enough time to go back to his house and have a quickie. My head wasn't really computing what he was saying. I mumbled, "No, it's ok," which sent him into a tizzy about how no one says no to him. He said he was hot and could have anyone he wanted, anytime he wanted. And besides, he could do better than . . ."

I think the last word was “me,” but by that time, I was hurrying out the door.

Date #44
Mr. Squeak.

One of the many problems with online dating is that you never know what to expect. You really don't know if the person will be older, fatter, thinner, shorter, taller, or anything else. I arranged to meet a clean-cut executive at a local bar for one drink in-between some kind of kid activity, which included the drop off and pick up of said kid. I had had yet another of those crazy here, there, and everywhere days that single working parents often have.

I rolled into the bar. He's sitting right in front. He's actually surprisingly more handsome in person than in his photos. I sit down, introduce myself and he says his name. As he goes to ask me what I would like to drink, out of his mouth, there is a very high pitch squeak, followed by a twitch in his eye.

Initially I ignore it, as I'm not sure if it was strange hiccup or something. I answer vodka soda, and then I ask him how his day was. "It was squeak pretty busy squeak. Which sends me into a fit of giggles. I, at times, find humor in very inappropriate things and moments. I am that person who just might laugh at a bit of humor at a funeral, or laugh when someone falls down on *America's Funniest Home Videos*. The less appropriate it is means the harder I laugh.

I try to regain my composure. The poor guy says nothing. No explanation, but keeps talking and squeaking. Every time I think it's stopped, another squeak appears. This sends me right back to fits of giggles. Not like little snickers, but like cheek hurting-eyes watering uncontrollable laughter. I excuse myself to go to the rest room. I have by now deduced that he has some kind of nervous tick or something, and I am wondering both why he didn't say anything before we met and also why, as I am sat in front of him being ridiculously impropriate, he hasn't said anything.

I go back to bar and, bless him, he's still sitting there politely smiling. We somehow finish the drink and I am relieved I have to go. He walks me to the car and asks to meet for dinner the following day. I politely decline, driving away wondering why so many people don't disclose things before showing up. I am pretty sure this guy was a super good guy who, if he shared that with people beforehand, wouldn't have to deal with girls like me crying and laughing through the date.

9

Educating Tiffany

I was never the best student at school. I was far more interested in my outfit choice for the day than in the content of any lesson or lecture. I was lucky enough to attend some pretty decent schools, graduate from college and come to the USA to work at my first big girl job. In my jubilation, I had forgotten that I really had no clue what I was doing or any knowledge of anything tech or website-related. I think in many ways ignorance was bliss; I just presumed it couldn't be that hard to "figure out." What I was about to embark on over the next few months was a 24/7 emergence into the world of online business. Which, for a female over 35 with no computer or business knowledge, was no small undertaking.

I had no idea even where to start except for knowing that I needed - a web designer to build my website. A few quick Googles for web designers led me to a website called Elance.com, one of those website where you can post a job and a plethora of people and companies bid for your job. The great thing about the web and hiding behind a keyboard is it not only makes you brave for online dating but also in business,

I posted my web site job description, feeling like a fraud. How would I know what I wanted? Would I even understand any of the terms? Luckily for me the Enlace community seemed none too put off by my total lack of tech knowledge. In a list of tech descriptions, mine read something like "website with marketplace for individuals to sell items to individuals." That was it. I literally couldn't fill out the format or specs stuff. I had become a stay-at-home mom who had spent most of the last decade cleaning up after kids, dogs, and men.

Within a few days I had bids. It was actually quite exciting, people wanted to build my website and thought they could. And even better, the bids were all between two and five thousand dollars, which I figured I could find somehow. I set up my very first business calls with three of the perspective web design companies. Even just being able to do this was exhilarating and felt empowering after so many years of feeling powerless.

After I had spoken to all three companies, I wired 50% of the money to Elance, and I officially became a girl with a tech start-up under development. I sent them website designs I liked and picked out the colors for my company, hot pink and turquoise, because what's not to feel upbeat about with those bright cheerful colors? I began to put myself on a work schedule, I took my kids to school, worked out for an hour, then began educating myself. Thank goodness for the World Wide Web, you can literally find anything you want, all free, right at your figure tips,

Firstly I looked up ecommerce/ marketplaces. I read everything and anything I could about them - how commission works, listing fees, PayPal payments, credit card processing, liability and on and on. Then over the next four months, I read, and this is not an exaggeration, about 10 hours a day. During the other six I was awake, I was dealing with my children and house. I read until one or two a.m. every night and woke up at 5.30 to take the kids to school.

I was book marking articles and making notes. I was teaching myself SEO, social media, marketing, branding, ecommerce, blogging, adaptive payments, Florida business laws, and much more. You name it, I was inhaling it. I was still living on coffee and cheese mostly and my bum had begun to wear a flat spot in the kitchen booth cushion where I parked myself from morning to night. If you have seen the movie *Limitless,* it was like a more realistic version of that - downloading a ridiculous amount of information that was all entirely new to me into my now thirsty sponge-like brain. A brain that was extremely interested in all this new information but was apparently being awakened from the non-mental stimulation of being a stay at home mom. I was tired, but I was so starting to feel happy.

During this period, my financial situation was still as dismal as ever. Repairs to my 12-year old car seemed endless. There were endless broken home items. My electricity was turned off twice. I scrambled to borrow money from one thing to pay for another thing. Every time I started to get finances in a little better order - something else would happen, a medical bill for my kids, a broken-down car, another unexpected bill. I non-affectionately call these the "screw my life years." Anything and everything seemed to be working against me still. I was working on the website like a crazy woman, eager to prove everyone wrong, but it didn't stop life continuing to hard pitch lemons at me randomly. The great thing though, was I was coping a lot better. An occurrence that used to send me retreating into my cocoon bed for 3-4-5-11 days now would maybe make me shed a few tears of frustration and move on. It also would propel me back to the computer to educate myself even more. I had shifted my mindset from a victim to a fighter, and I was not going to let anyone or anything beat me.

I was inadvertently not just thinking, but *living* the life that Simon had advocated. He had planted the seed very deeply in my mind that all energies should only be directed at things you can change, control, or work towards, and that's what I was doing all day, every day. I went from having conversations with my web team in which I had to ask them to explain every term and technical jargon used to as actually discussing with them the pros and cons of what code to use to build the website. I was not tech savvy yet but I was gaining business and tech knowledge in what I thought I wanted to accomplish with *DreamsRecycled* and the plan of how I was going to do this had begun to take shape.

Simon was as supportive as ever, celebrating every step with me - finding the web designers, the color choices, and the logo I badly doodled on my children's homework. He was my biggest cheerleader and just having him to talk to regarding business things was invaluable. Plus, I needed him to correct my atrocious spelling errors and to forbid me from using "of" instead of "have," his pet peeve. He was my anchor in the storm that still was turbulent on most days. That's the thing about divorce. When you have 16 years of life to untangle and three children together, it takes quite a while. And the road to serenity is paved with landmines you often don't even see coming.

The website was to be ready 90 days from the start, but I had a million and one things to do on my end to get it ready, namely content. What is a marketplace without items? I also had to stockpile blogs about divorce to add to my blog section, I was instantly a blogger. I presumed no one would read them, so I just actually wrote blogs and articles I thought would have been helpful to me during my divorce. I was discovering that despite what I had been brainwashed to believe by some people, I was actually ok at a lot of things, I was writing blogs that I think were pretty informative, I was successfully collaborating on my website build with designers. I had set up at the time five social media pages, *Facebook, Pinterest, Twitter, Instagram,* and *Google*. I apparently wasn't so untrainable or non-skilled as I thought, or had been told.

The business side of my life was restoring my faith and confidence in myself, little by little. Everything I managed to do by myself and everything I checked off my long daily lists went a little way to healing my shattered ego, and self-esteem that were the parting gifts of my divorce. I still had a long way to go, but I was definitely headed in the right direction.

I was fortunate in my circle of friends to be able to ask and, more importantly, receive help from a few amazing friends. I was having trouble finding hours in the day and the website needed items. It also needed a logo and photos. Randy was a friend of mine from the gym, and a parent of my daughter's friend. He was also a graphic artist, I swallowed my pride, because asking for anything isn't my forte, and he very kindly agreed to create a logo for me. He also went above and beyond with getting a photographer friend of his, Eric Dean, to agree to take photos for the website's home page.

Next thing you know, I was washing another friend's Ferrari, in a wedding dress and veil, having my photos taken, which was actually extremely liberating. I was trashing my wedding dress, having fun in the process, I had had my hair and makeup done and I was feeling somewhat pretty which for me, was a vast improvement. Eric was great. I had also roped my lovely sister-in-law, Rebecca, my good friend, Jennifer, who was a great sport and unboxed her wedding dress to use, too, and, of course, Nancy who loves any excuse to dress up, to have their photos taken too. It was a great fun day and I was incredibly grateful for their help. We left with a great set of shots of everyone and the home page banner ad photo that was an accident.

I had trashed the wedding dress. I was soaking wet and as we were about to wrap up, I had this idea of taking the trashed dress off and laying it over the car and sitting on the wet floor in front of the car. Eric and Randy thought I was nuts, no doubt, but went along with it anyway. I sat in my knickers on the wet floor behind a friend's luxury car with my girlfriends supporting me. In that moment, someone said something funny, I laughed out loud, and Eric got the best shot of the day. Me laughing, happy and relieved that somehow, I would survive this divorce. Not just survive but thrive, and if any photo tells a thousand words, that one did. It is still circulating the Internet; I'm certainly no model but the joy it captures I think people relate to.

Back at my house, over the next few weeks, my incredible giving friends were there to help. Jennifer, Randy, and Melissa were there to help, collecting items for the marketplace. We begged, borrowed, and ok, we didn't steal, but we all worked to gather items like wedding dresses and rings from anyone we could think of. It was amazing how many divorcees, many years after their divorce, still had their wedding items. They never knew what to do with them and were happy to find a place to sell them off. Which only went to validate that this was a pretty good idea. Of course, we hadn't launched yet and as much as I believed in this idea, I was also concerned that maybe no one would like it, or use it on mass scale. Who knew -there was nothing like it so I wasn't sure what the launch would bring.

I was still working insane hours, which now included photographs and listing on excel sheets the hundreds and hundreds of divorce items we collected. When we opened, our marketplace had things to sell. I had stockpiled 20 or so blogs on divorce related topics, and Randy had taken my balloon idea and made it into a beautiful pink and turquoise logo. It was starting to look, feel and seem like an actual business was taking shape. A pretty interesting groundbreaking one at that.

Those ninety days flew by. I never had a day in which I worked less than 16-20 hours. I was exhausted. I was also sneaking in odd date here and there when I just needed a diversion, but mostly those months, were all work and no play. I didn't mind. When you find something you are passionate about, a calling as such, work doesn't seem too bad. And I was extremely grateful to the universe for the dream that was about to become reality.

Date #94
Mr. Math

I have been on a few *one and done* dates with models, actor types. They are sometimes super smart and well educated, sometimes not so much. So I show up at this French restaurant for a date with an actor/ model. He's incredible gorgeous in his photos, so much so that I made him jump through a ton of identity-proving hoops to even meet me.

He is probably the only person I have been on a date with who made me feel a little insecure about my looks. I like to be the pretty one on a date, not the man. Anyway, we are sharing a bottle of wine. He is a sweet as can be. His conversation is nice yet not far reaching.

We start to discuss his work and where he has to travel. He tells me that he does a lot of work on the West Coast, and NYC. I can imagine he does. He's incredibly handsome. I ask him which he prefers, NYC or LA? This is his answer: *I like NYC better because when you fly to LA, going there it's three hours, but the eight hour flight back is just way too long*. Hmmmmm No Words...bless him.

10

Let's Talk About Press Baby!

With the launch fast approaching, I had been able to scrape together a little more money to invest in a local PR firm. I really was just thinking that maybe they could do a press release and if I was lucky someone might see it and it drive a few people to my site. I brought my friend Jennifer down town to meet with the PR firm, Vantage. They were personable and helpful and if they realized I was totally clueless about how PR actually worked, they were kind enough to not let on. I dragged out a work dress I had from a decade ago (thank God wrap dresses never go out of style), put on a pair of stilettos which were a far cry from the sneakers I wore most days, and sat in the meeting looking like I knew what I wanted.

My story is real, so it basically wrote itself for the PR team to pitch. *A single mom of three children dreams she can't sell her engagement ring, and during the dream she has an epiphany that she can sell her ring and the rings of everyone else on a website called DreamsRecycled.*

By anyone's standards, it is a pretty interesting story and has the element of turning lemons into lemonade. That is a story that is universally loved. The meeting went well and the press release was prepared for launch. The day of the launch was coming nearer. I had picked July 7th as launch day. If you've been keeping up, you know it was because I have both had a lifelong obsession with the number 7 and it seemed lucky that in fact the website was actually due to be ready that week anyway.

My web team was sending me development website updates constantly and I could see my site coming together. The hot pink and the mostly white looked pretty. It was starting to look totally like a marketplace as they had begun to load all the items. Pretty cool I have to say. I would wake up most mornings and pinch myself that I had even got this far from a dream, I had actually changed my life in the 7 seconds it took me to make the decision to actually do this business to become an entrepreneur. It literally was the hardest decision of my life but also in many ways the easiest. When you believe in an idea or thought so much, actually doing it becomes pretty simple.

The PR, team headed by Katie and Laura, had been great and we were ready to launch, whatever launch really meant in the tech world, I was about to have my website go live and see my name go out into cyber land as the CEO of my own tech start up. It was all about to get very, very real.

Date #112
Dr Love.

I gravitate towards successful, well-educated, worldly men maybe because I'm British, but it means that I have been on many, many a date with lawyers and doctors of all kinds. I have dated entomologists, cardiologists, anesthesiologists, gastroenterologists, pediatricians, emergency room physicians and a plethora of chiropractors, who I am never really sure if they are doctors.

My favorite doctor story by far is a guy I met who was cute in an edgy kind of way. He had a bunch of tattoos, which I secretly kind of like when they are well done and thought out. Who doesn't have a bad boy thing ever so often?

Well, we met for lunch by his hospital, and he showed up in scrubs, another kind of hot look on a man, and we had a super nice time. He was sweet, kind, and funny. We arranged to go out to dinner later in the week. Dinner came and went without much excitement and we strolled back to his house. Once inside he put on some music and started to kiss me, a kiss that turned to a kiss with serious hip swaying, slight dirty dancing, to all-of-a-sudden-out-of-nowhere, an entire Chippendale strip show. He had apparently paid for his entire medical degree by stripping. Pretty impressive on his dedication, I must say.

Date #205
Mr. Honest.

I like people. I like their stories, their quirks. I am always interested in people when I meet them. I also have mass empathy for most souls. I am fascinated when I learn anything new from anyone.

I met a man the same age as me for coffee. The same age means young for me. I prefer to date men 10-15 years older than me. Not really sure why. I just do. The man is lovely. He, too, is a divorced single parent. As I am talking to him I can sense he's going to get something off his chest.

"Tiffany," he says, "I have to tell you I am a recovering alcoholic, I received another person's liver which changed my personality." We sat outside Starbucks and discussed in depth his alcoholism and subsequent transplant and how this had affected his life, his health and his persona. I remember thinking. "Wow, he's brave to share all of that on a first date." But he was too young for me and I chose not to see him again. He was a reminder how we are all flawed, all have some kind of baggage, and we should all just come clean about it up front to save ourselves and others the fallout from thinking we have been deceived. Honesty really is the best policy.

11

July 7th 2013 Launch

I had spoken to Simon and he had approved 7/7 as the launch day. His birthday also lies on a seven. The website had actually been up for a week or so but clearly no one knew it existed, We were shooing out the bugs, loading more blogs and last minute items we had gathered. While working with the web team, they had treated me as I was - a mom with a little website that no one would visit. The website was fine but small on scale and bandwidth. This would come back to bite us later.

I awoke on the seventh with mass anxiety but also a sense of extreme accomplishment. My website had to work which meant that people had to like my idea to make it a viable business. On a personal level, I had achieved the unthinkable. If anyone in those few years during my dark depression had told me I was going to educate myself on IT, incorporate my company, and with 90 days, go from unemployable to CEO, I would have told them unequivocally that they were out of their mind. Tiffany couldn't possibly do that. So unlike me, I would have said. Yet here I was, ninety days later, with the help from a few amazing friends, a few thousand dollars, an unyielding work ethic, and newfound ambition. I had achieved so much. It was mind boggling to me, I was grateful. I was overwhelmed. But it had all been so worth it if only from the point of view of rebuilding my belief in my own worth and skills that had somehow been eradicated during my 16 year marriage.

On July seventh, with one click of the submit button, by my PR firm sent out a press release that would change my life forever. More changes than I expected. My regular life was still in full swing. Within days after the press release had gone out, I received a call from Laura asking if I wanted to be interviewed for a tiny segment on the local Fox News 35 in Orlando. Sure, I said, thinking, *Oh, that will be nice. Maybe a few neighbors may see it.*

The PR Company had also lined up a couple of interviews with some local news organizations. I was excited. I had never done press at all. I wasn't particularly comfortable with being on camera, but I was committed to doing whatever I needed to do to make my business a success.

I also gave a couple of phone interviews over the next few weeks. People had in very small numbers begun visiting the website. Items were being listed here and there. It was a slow start and I was ok with that since we were still taking care of some glitches. I started posting daily on social media. A few people started looking. So there was movement, but very little.

The day came for the Fox News interview. They had been insistent that they film inside my house, which caused even more anxiety since I had to sort out the disaster it had become from working 80 hour weeks and having no time to clean it. I found a dress that seemed ok at the time. I took my kids to school, then jumped in the shower. I certainly didn't have time to fix or style my hair and was downstairs to greet the crew in my house by 10 a.m. I had the foresight to throw on a little make up, but truly all I kept thinking was, Try not to say anything stupid. But also running through my mind was, *Don't worry if you do since hardly anyone will see this, anyway.*

The interview went ok. I spoke about turning lemons into lemonade. I stood in my family room in a turquoise dress and smiled awkwardly as I tried not to mess up too much. Thank goodness they let me say things multiple times. It was over I crawled back into my workout clothes and went about my business being a single mom.

The segment aired in the evening. I was relieved to see that it had been edited to make me seem knowledgeable on my business and what I wanted to achieve with it. It was a short, interesting local news story. As soon as it aired I watched as my website numbers spiked. It was exciting to see tens of thousands of people visit us. I received my first few emails through the contact form, saying how much they loved my business idea. I also received a string of texts from local friends who had no idea what I was doing, congratulating me on an awesome idea. I was really happy about that part since without people who also believed in it, I it would not be a viable business.

The next day I was driving through McDonalds for my unsweet ice tea addiction, when all of a sudden my phone started to ping, not just one ping, but random alerts. It was the sound of the DreamsRecycled email. I thought that was odd and as I looked down and opened my phone, I started to cry. Dozens and dozens of wedding and divorce items were listed. Dozens of accounts had been opened, one after the other. They were tears of joy, the virtual proof that people not only liked my idea, but also were willing to use it.

Remember, we aren't the only market place for this subject, but we are the only one specializing in divorce. My theory was correct. People were hanging on to their items as they didn't really know what to do with them. And when given DreamsRecycled as an option, they were choosing it. I got my tea, pulled over to a parking space and just sobbed. My children were at first concerned something else awful had happened, but when I explained what it was, they were happy too. Tilly had sympathy tears she smiled through. The boys I think were just grateful something else untoward hadn't happened. I went home, frantically texted Simon, telling him people were using it. He, of course, had no doubt they would.

Under the umbrella of being careful what you wish for, my little local Fox News story was about to become a global storm, I didn't realize at the time how local news could be picked up for syndication nationwide, but I quickly learned the hard way. So what I thought was going to be me with untamed hair, being seen by few local people turned into me with untamed hair being possibly seen by any human who watches Fox News anywhere. I knew this had happened because I checked my website and it had crashed. The last spike we recorded was 130,000 unique visitors on one day. I frantically called the web team who worked on putting it back up. When they did put it back up few hours later, it went down again. That time it was 150,000 unique visitors on one day. We were not prepared for this technically and I was not prepared for what was coming next.

Huffington Post is the largest online news source in the world. They had seen my Fox News piece go national and had made it into a cool video blog and story. Which was then also used as the opening video story on AOL worldwide. If I tried to explain exactly the effect this had on my company and opportunities, I couldn't and still can't. I will say, though, that I will forever be grateful to Fox News and Huffington Post for giving my company this kind of global exposure. Huffington Post UK version also created a great short video on my company that they also featured worldwide.

I was getting my 15 minutes of fame in a spectacular way. I couldn't believe it. Within days, I had over half a million people visit my website. Think about that. It blew my mind that so many people liked it. My mail box was slammed with hundreds, maybe thousands, of messages from other divorcees who were congratulating me or encouraging me or asking for more blogs, chat rooms or divorce services. Within six weeks of launch, we had become a viable company and a media sensation.

I was surprised at how many people connected with me personally and how many people wanted to share their divorce stories with me. I was also surprised that from Day One, 50% of our users were male. There was clearly an overwhelming need for a positive way to deal with divorce. There was also an overwhelming demand from people, media, radio, bloggers, and magazines to hear more of my story and journey. I never once thought that I would be the face or poster child for divorce. It isn't something you grow up thinking about. I was honored, excited, and in some ways a little scared of being thrust into the media spotlight. I was still struggling with my own feelings, and waiting for someone to jump out and tell me I had been pranked.

I was fielding calls from major TV networks about having my own TV show. Book publishers wanted my story. Film producers from Los Angeles called. People wanted me to speak publicly. My PR team fielded most of the requests for interviews. Within a few weeks, I was in multiple publications, I was on dozens of radio shows, and I had dozens of would-be investors wanting to buy into my company. I wasn't sure what had happened in such a small amount of time. Six months before this I was practically unable to get out of bed. Now major news outlets wanted to hear my story. It felt amazing in a million ways. I had hope I was being validated, which was amazing, but I was also apprehensive as I tried to navigate my radical life changes.

My life now consisted of photo shoots, interviews, network calls, listening to divorce stories, trying at times unsuccessfully to get my website to accommodate the ongoing spikes, and keep up with each child's school activities. The tech part in some ways became the hardest part to navigate. It was the only part I couldn't actually do myself.

I think my kids were also on a media high. They kept walking around the house saying, "Are you famous now, mom? Why do people want to talk to you all the time?"

"Can we get a zip line?" became a common theme, because, after all, they are just kids. But they seemed happy, hopeful and most certainly extremely glad that my migraines and sleep time had become almost nonexistent.

I navigated my way through the next few months in a blur of activity, firsts and excitement. I did my first radio show. I was on the front page of my first newspaper. I met with the first of eleven investors. I interviewed for my first national magazine. It was beyond my wildest expectations, and I had to pinch myself many times over this time frame. The weirdest part was the nagging thought in my head that what if I hadn't had followed my dream? I would still have been an unemployable, stay-at-home mom. It was an awful lot, in a small amount of time, to wrap my head around. I was crazy busy, and I needed a vacation and I knew exactly who I wanted to spend it with.

Date #354
Mr. Scary Scammer.

Online dating is actually very dangerous; I learned very quickly that you Google everyone and you always meet in a very public, open place. You never allow anyone to pick you up, or go to their house on a first date.

One look at any news source will confirm this. I have, over time, become an expert at researching potential dates. From a simple Google search, I have found people to be married (this doesn't always show though), to have long criminal records, to have been arrested for soliciting prostitutes, domestic violence charges, and on and on. The Internet brings you unlimited options and with it, untold dangers.

As good as I have become, some still slip through the net, I was contacted by a so-called "plastic surgeon." He seemed ok, nothing dramatically off about him or his profile. We agreed to meet for lunch locally. He arrived. I arrived. We sat down, and he gave me a lot of compliments, on my looks, clothes and shoes. We ordered lunch. I began to ask him about his work, what kind of plastic surgery did he specialize in? He answered each question briefly, but quickly followed with, "But let's not talk about me. I want to know all about you."

As the meal went on I realized he was really deflecting any questions I asked, I had managed to extract from him that he had two children and was divorced after a long marriage, and he loved to travel. He quizzed me on my life; I too shared as little as possible. At one point he asked if my ex and I were ever swingers or liked threesomes, which was little out there for first meeting. I tried again to steer conversation back to him and his work. I started to realize that something was off. I have never met a doctor who doesn't like to talk about himself, especially a plastic surgeon.

I debated whether to leave right then, but we were almost done with lunch. The waiter brought the check. He opened his wallet and as he slid out his credit card to pay I saw on it a totally different name than the one he had given me. My eyes scanned the other credit card face up in wallet, same as first credit card name.

He asked me to join him in the Bahamas that weekend. He was scaring me at this point, and I was running through my head, why someone would lie about who and what he was and then expect you to go away for the weekend with him?

It couldn't be good. I declined and said I had to go I was late, I ran to my car and sat in the parking lot, I wanted to make sure he left before me and there was no way he could follow me home. He walked out. I crouched down in my car. He got into a beat up Honda civic and drove away. There are a lot of fake profiles and people with deceitful at the best and sinister at the worst intentions. Women, too, have ulterior motives and are often scammers. Be vigilant, be safe.

12

Hong Kong Fooey

I have loved to travel for my entire life. As a child growing up in England, I was fortunate that my family traveled regularly through Europe and North America. As an adult, though, after my move to the USA, I had mostly only had the opportunity to travel within the country. Drowning in small children, and having no money of my own made it impossible to do.

I had always wanted to go to Asia. It seemed like the farthest, most diverse place to go, and it was also where Simon happened to live. DreamsRecycled had given me belief in myself and wings to fly higher and farther away than ever before. I was the kind of mom who had a hard time leaving her kids even for a school day. But through my divorce journey, I had realized that being a martyr for your kids is not such a great way to be. It hadn't made me any better of a parent, and I found reluctantly as my kids started spending time with their dad, that I really needed my time alone and with other adults.

The guilt lasted longer than the alone time did, but I was coping with both and figured if I didn't have my children for Thanksgiving that year, anyway, I might as well go cross something off my bucket list. I could see someone who meant a lot to me at the same time. I also could buy bulk wedding dresses to fill up some space on DreamsRecycled's website. I booked my ticket and told Simon, who I am pretty sure was as nervous as I was, about our upcoming meeting, meeting after a million texts, and a 35-year old crush.

I like flying. Well I thought I did until I flew to Hong Kong. After a three hour flight to Chicago and a two hour layover I was seated next to a large man on a 16 hour, 50 min direct flight to Hong Kong. After the first

10 hours, I was ready to claw myself out of the window. The worst part was realizing I had both claustrophobia and also a hatred of other random humans' breath, smell, heat, incessant talking and germs. Really, I am not very crowd friendly. So I arrive in Hong Kong at the JW Marriott in total exhaustion, realizing I have not slept or eaten for about three days. I am semi aware of people looking at me but I just figure I looked like a wreck and maybe they feel bad for me, I stumble into my room, and pass out for the next 14 hours waking starving at 7 am, in desperate search of food.

Before my marriage I was a fashion lover, dressing on the cutting edge, stylishly sexy, a little like a hippy in heels. My mommy life had somehow morphed into a Gap khaki Capri, white t-shirt, and sandal-wearing robot. In hindsight I am not sure what I was thinking. Maybe that baby puke showed less on khakis, hard to tell. What I *did* know though was one of the most radical changes I made in my personal life after my divorce, even before DreamsRecycled, was that I went back to wearing stylish, sexy, fun clothes, clothes that made me happy, and feel like a woman, not a house elf in servitude to small humans.

My vacation wardrobe consisted of bright mini dresses, hot sexy dresses, and a business ensemble to meet with wedding dress manufactures. I wake up, throw on a bright red dress with a full short skirt and some cowboy boots. I hurry to the lobby in search of food. Again, I am aware that everyone is looking at me. I get in the elevator and am starving and feeling slightly faint. The elevator opens into the dining room with a few steps down into the buffet area and then the large open plane area of tables. I practically fall out the elevator in my bright red dress and as I walk out, suddenly am acutely aware that the room has become very silent. I look around the room packed with a mixture of expats and Asians. I realize I am the only female there, especially the only one dressed in a mini dress and cowboy boots at 7 am.

The host greets me and I ask what is wrong. Why is everyone looking at me? He says it's just because there are not many white businesswomen alone in Hong Kong. It was definitely odd, like scene out a movie. It was also a good indicator of what my entire trip would be like. Simon was meeting me for the last three days, which gave me some time to sleep and explore the area alone, another thing I thought I would never enjoy. But I did. Traveling alone is a great way to learn about other cultures, countries and also a great way to learn about yourself. It forces you to be friendlier than usual, to trust others more, to learn to like your own company, and find value in yourself. I loved every single minute of everything I did. I met an amazing lady called Amy who was the owner of the wedding dress manufacturing facility. After I picked out some dresses from her, she insisted on taking me for a real Hong Kong adventure through the streets of Kowloon in search of a lucky cat for my daughter who had requested one as a trip souvenir. Another time, I was sitting in a Starbucks, trying to navigate a subway map, when two lively expats bought me a drink and insisted on hand delivering me to the correct place on the subway so I didn't get lost. I must have really looked like a bimbo in person, but it was sweet and I found the country amazing, the people lovely, and the atmosphere friendly. Everywhere I went, I was invited places, or joined for dinner or drinks.

Simon arrived on time and I stayed in my hotel room in anxious anticipation, I couldn't even believe I was going to see him. A thousand, million thoughts of him over 35 years, combined with thousands of texts, hundreds of tears and a trillion little butterflies landing in my stomach. I must have changed 14 times. What do you wear after three decades? He texted *I'm here* and I opened the hotel door just in time to see him, walking down the hallways, his eyes as blue as the first day I met him at elementary school, his sandy hair as tussled as then, also. He had grown into a handsome six-foot, one-inch successful entrepreneur and a highly educated businessman. But to me, he was still the little boy on the bike who was brave enough to ride alone to knock on my door to see if I could come outside and play with him. The boy brave enough to leave me a scribbled *I love you* note. It was actually little too much reality as we stood there awkwardly. After separating from a far too long hug, we moved into a weird silence. Before it could get any weirder I suggested we head straight to pre-dinner drinks to talk.

We sat in the bar area, ordered a couple drinks and within a few minutes felt much less nervous. We once again fell into our childhood ways, teasing each other, talking too much. Only now it was over Hendricks and vodkas, not over popsicles and sodas. We walked over to the stunning roof top restaurant, Sevva, and the night began to take on a magical feel. I was a million miles from Orlando, with one of my best friends and biggest supporters. I was in a stunning restaurant with thousands of flowers hanging from the ceiling, and there were pink lit Christmas trees lit all over the balcony, for the upcoming holidays. I let Simon order an array of amazing exotic foods. We discussed everything and anything, both of us aware that our time together was limited, trying to somehow fill each other in on decades of life and funny stories. We laughed, confided and bonded, but most of all, enjoyed each other's company. After dinner, we headed to a club called Tonic where he held my hand tightly so I didn't bust my ass on the cobblestones in 4-inch heels. Or run off with any of the other men there who were on the prowl. We danced, drank, and laughed our way through the night.

On arrival back at the hotel, I realized Simon hadn't let go of my hand all evening. He had instantly morphed back into his protective mode of me he had since we were seven. The door closed behind us as Simon leaned forward to kiss me, not the way seven year olds kiss but the way two adults who deeply care for each other kiss. We were channeling three decades of flirting thoughts, love and kindness into this moment.

We kissed, for the first time as adults, his hands on my face. We loved each other in a way, and on many levels that I think don't really make sense to others. It wasn't about owning each other, or being together, it was about a genuine unconditional love, that usually you can only get to over a long trusting period of time.

I think it is very easy to see why so many people after divorce reconnect with various exes and loved ones from their childhood, school days or college. It feels safe, it's familiar and it is comforting to your battered heart. Especially, I think, when your trust in others has been shattered, these past loves seem like a safe port in the emotional storm of divorce. Simon, my funny, witty, brilliant friend, who took time, thought and care in babysitting me from the other side of the world (and on a twelve hour time difference), had still been there every step of the way, virtually holding my hand, and making sure I was ok.

Simon and I knew we couldn't actually have a relationship in real life, but it didn't stop us caring for one another deeply. Quite frankly, at this time I also wouldn't have been ready for a great love affair, as much as I wanted one. My heart and soul still needed to heal and I certainly, although coming much further in my journey, hadn't mastered self-love in full. It was, though, amazing to see someone who was my supporter, my best friend, and protector, in real life. And he felt like a million things, the two most important of which were safe and trustworthy.

The next few days we spent sightseeing and shopping, and as it drew closer to the day we both left, I started to realize just how very far we actually were from each other. Simon had told me he never felt as big as loss as when he said goodbye to me at 10 years of age. Now, again we were in a position of having to say goodbye, not knowing if we would ever see each other again. The few last hours of the day, were a blur of heartache, tears, but no promises. Just more an acceptance that this may well be the last time we would be in the same place. We hugged in the airport by the train. He had to go one way, I the other. Tears streamed down my face as we held each other for the last time. I managed to mutter goodbye and he actually refused to even say those words, and just walked away.

I had another 24 hours of travel ahead of me and the rest of the holidays to navigate my way through with kids, business and investor meetings. It still seemed crazy to me that one little local TV interview had snowballed into random people from all over the world wanting to invest in DreamsRecycled. I was deeply saddened, leaving Simon but I also knew that the best plan of distraction is always action. I was going to throw myself once again into working 20-hour days, to achieve all the things I now had faith I actually could do. Simon had become my restorer in faith in mankind that week and maybe that alone was worth the trip.

Date #254
Mr. Fertility Checker.

I know that scientists have long said we subconsciously pick our mates on what we perceive their reproductive health to be. I made the mistake of agreeing to a date with a man who was a single parent to a teenager. He was some kind of banker. Upon meeting him, he seemed normal. No red flags. He looked like his photos. We sat at a high top table in a sports bar, ordered food and a drink. He then launched into the kind of standard dating interview you get – *where are you from? do you have siblings? how old are your children?* So far pretty standard fare.

Can I see photos of you children? He asked as he jammed a photo of his child in my face. "Cute," I said, I don't show people photos of my kids on first dates. It's a little creepy to me. I lied and said I didn't have any on my phone. *Oh that's a shame,* he said. *Are they all healthy?* I told him they were. *Do they look like you?* I told him they did. *Have you had natural childbirth?* I am concerned about these questions, but there's more. *Are your tubes tied?* he said. *Can you still have children?*

I laugh. "I'm sorry." I'm confused by this line of questioning."

He immediately gets both aggressive and defensive. *Well I want to have more children and if your uterus doesn't work, then you aren't much good to me.*

I actually am lost for words, which rarely happens to me. I in-form him that my uterus works perfectly well but it won't ever be working for him, I stand up and leave.

13

Investors

If my divorce had taught me anything, it was that it is a lot easier to attach your name to someone than detach it from someone. It takes approximately 10 minutes in a court house to be affixed to each other legally in marriage, but it somehow took me over four years of utter misery to detach myself legally and financially from someone. This thought played heavily in my head. I was under no illusion that taking money from someone as an investor would mean that I was also a partner for life with this person. It was not something I really wanted to do I had only been divorced a few months and the thought of seeing my name on any paper work with anyone else's filled me with fear.

Divorce is an interesting beast, it takes things from you that you wanted to hold on to, and it also gives you things you never wanted, like serious self-doubt. My divorce had left me with an overwhelming doubt in my ability to judge other humans. I think one of the stages of divorce is always a moment where you look back and internally shake your head with large sigh of "I don't even know who that was I married." There is often a feeling that you were married to either people you have no idea about, or that you were somehow married to someone that radically changed. And now, you were left wondering if anything during your years together was even real. I had reached this stage very early in my own separation, and dating Marcus hadn't done an awful lot to restore my faith in my good judgment of others.

On the business side, though, I had become aware that the website we had up was not going to be good enough or big enough long term to deal with the traffic and all the additional things I wanted to add now for our users. I also wanted to create a new website that I knew could scale as we moved into Canada and UK. This would take money, six-figure money. And even though the website was buzzing with traffic and transactions were being made at a 7% commission, it wasn't enough. With overhead and marketing DreamsRecycled needed money. So I decided to quiet my fears and hope that in the pool of would-be investors would be someone both trustworthy, kind and business savvy.

My first potential investors reminded me a little of a *Shark Tank* episode. They just wanted flat out equity for barely any money. I declined these people, and another four business men who I will say where lower end speculators, hoping I guess to either get a huge portion of my company for hardly any money or even, I believe, a couple of them actually wanted to have sex in exchange for investment money. Neither of which I was willing to do.

By far the worst investor was a successful tech start-up guy, slightly younger than me, who flew in to for a dinner meeting at the Ritz Carlton. I drove to meet him and we had a wonderful dinner, discussing all aspects of, scaling, traffic, ecommerce, and tech start up investments. I naively thought it was going great. He randomly had pulled out a $400,000 investment figure, and we were discussing terms. I was getting excited that he could actually be the one. He clearly knew his stuff, way more than me. He said he was willing to be fully onboard, I was buzzing with excitement.

It was getting late and I had to drive home. He politely had taken care of the check, and we were wrapping up our intense business discussion. I reached into my bag and pulled out my valet parking ticket to validate it, when he said, "You don't need that. You can leave your car in valet for the evening. I got us a room."

My head began to spin. Why did he say us? Maybe he meant two rooms, as in he got us rooms, so I didn't have to drive home. We stood up to walk to the lobby and I asked him what he meant. Without missing a beat, he said, "Well if we are going to work together, we should seal the deal."

My blood pressure started to rise, and not in a good way. Did this idiot really think I was going to have sex with him for money? As calmly as possible, I explained I was not that person and walked to the valet, leaving him standing in the lobby. A lump formed in my throat from anger. I may not have had a startup before, I may not have sold my company for hundreds of millions of dollars, but I did have a viable and worthy business model. That in itself was worthy of investing in, without needing to have the added value of sleeping with me. I drove home feeling disgusted and unfairly treated, and once again my ability to judge people had taken a serious beating.

I decided that from now on I would have much longer, in-depth conversations with potential investors before I met them. I set up long phone conversations with the remaining few potential investors. I weeded out a couple more who also seemed a lot more interested in what was under my clothes than in my executive summary. I was starting to see that being a woman in business came with an additional set of issues to navigate. I had also been, during this time, growing weary from men who contacted me, asking me whose company and idea it really was.

Mine I would reply, and they would seem disappointed that I didn't actually have some brilliant man behind it. I also was annoyed by the few men I had dated who had referred to my business as a hobby. Like I was knitting all day and not working so I should drop everything to answer their texts or go on dates with them. I can't imagine men speaking or thinking like this about other men in business.

Luckily though for every one misogynistic man there were actually 10 or more great supportive business men who had seen me in some media outlet and had emailed or called to offer support or help. These men more than made up for the poor treatment a few had shown. One such man was a Swiss gentleman who had heard of my company through some other investors on the west coast. He sent an email asking to speak about potential investment opportunities. I spoke with him and as far as I could tell, he seemed fine. Not just fine but actually brilliant in IQ and EQ a rare combo. He was one of those men who although being ridiculously well educated and successful, never once spoke down to me. We discussed divorce, suicide, and murder rates in USA. I shared with him some of my personal divorce story and he said he would like to meet on his next trip to Florida. I didn't have high hopes. People had begun to form a pattern of being disappointing to me, so I just agreed and continued also speaking with multiple other potential domestic investors.

Date #4
Mr. Octopus.

Date number 4 was the date that made me realize you shouldn't go on a dinner date with anyone you have never met. This man was a scientist of sorts, very intelligent, IQ wise, but seriously lacking EQ wise. At dinner he insisted on sitting next to me in the booth, which is lovely *only* when you know someone. He then proceeded to order dinner for me, which, if he *knew* me, might be ok.

As we waited for dinner, he transformed into an eight-armed octopus. He ran his finger over my bare arm, which made me flinch. I pulled away but there is only so far you can go when jammed into the end of a booth. He continued, alternating between trying to rest his hand on my thigh, and trying to hold my hand. Both of which I verbally told him I was not comfortable with.

It was the longest, most uncomfortable dinner ever. I couldn't get far enough away from him and he seemed to have zero understanding of any body language or verbal cues I gave him. I wasn't responding. I certainly wasn't flirting. I had no interest in him. He was making my skin crawl. The purgatory of dinner finally ended and he insisted on walking me to my car. He tried to hug me. I thanked him for dinner and as I did, he darted forward, pulled me close, and stuck his tongue in the corner of my mouth, which was repulsive.

I pushed him away and he still had to no clue. Instead, he asked,

"Do you want to come back to my place now?"

I didn't even speak, I just left, fuming, but I never went on another first date to dinner again.

14

I am an Expert

During the next few months, I was busy working like a fiend on apps, marketing, social media, and various interviews. I was also fielding thousands of divorce questions. I was oddly not just becoming a tech start up CEO, but also a divorce expert. Each person's story I heard or read in an email was teaching me something, something I didn't know about human nature or divorce or even psychology. I was spending my evenings either dating or reading ridiculously in-depth articles on relationships, marriage, addictions, personality disorders, or psychology. It was fascinating, and went to prove my theory that truth is always stranger than fiction. I was submersing myself, little by little, in the divorce industry, reading laws, talking to family lawyers, therapists and life coaches, every person along the way was educating me on all things divorce.

It is amazing, when you hear thousands of divorce stories, how incredibly diverse they are, yet how common themes seem to dictate all of them. Literally through hearing so many divorce stories it became clear to me that divorce has three main factors that fuel it.

The first one is that whether we like to admit it or not, *people change and grow apart,* often falling out of love in the process. This kind of divorce is often the least tumultuous. People just agree to part ways, not that it makes aspects of it unpainful, or transition issues less traumatic. It just seems that one or both parties fall out of love, agreeing to divorce.

The second factor in divorce is that one or the other person *falls in love or starts to have a sexual or emotional affair* with another person. With stats as high as 87% of men admitting to cheating on a significant other and 67% of women admitting the same, this is clearly a large factor in divorce. I am loath to use the word "cause," as in the vast majority of cases, cheating is always only a symptom of other root causes within the demise of a marriage.

The last group of divorces I hear from a lot, I actually had no idea were so prevalent. This group consists of *anyone who either is or is married to someone with any kind of addiction, mental health issue or depression*. Over time, navigating the care, concerns, and issues that arise with these factors becomes too much within a marriage. Due to this being such a large group I also found it prudent to educate myself on all kinds of addictions, physical and emotional abuse, codependency, and the list goes on.

There really isn't anything as interesting as human behaviors and emotions. I found that I was not only educating myself to help others, but to understand *my* past relationships. No two people together have the same dynamic and unfortunately two great people can be horrible together, and two horrible people may, in fact, be great together. We are all flawed and wired from a very young age to act, think, expect, and desire things that are both healthy and unhealthy.

The quote that I think runs most true is that we all have baggage, even people who say they don't. Trying to blend any two flawed humans seamlessly into each other's life is a mixture of luck, love, and perseverance. Those who are strongest survive, and the rest sadly do not. No shame in this though. We all do the best we can with the cards dealt us. What counts much more along the way is realizing that in life, everything you do can be a positive or negative. Even in divorce it's all in how you view it. It can be the end of everything or the start of everything. I had made it my personal mantra to believe it was the later and go full force ahead with this theory.

During this time of having my mind immersed in divorce education and my days filled with talking to divorcees, something else magical was happening. With every act of helping others, or seeing them advance in their personal divorce journeys, they were propelling me in my own life. I was feeling, stronger, happier and more fulfilled each day. I was making friends and seeing my website usage increase. I was deriving more personal joy from giving than I ever had before. Although tired, I was sleeping again. I was feeling almost back to my old self, for which I was extremely grateful.

Date #48
Mr. Urine.

This date consisted of a man we will call Gary at first appearing very normal, attractive, and with a great smile. However after the first five minutes of polite greetings, he leaned over the table and with his face far too close to me (personal space please), he asked me if I could guess how many times he had “peed” today (and yes he used the word, “peed” in the first five minutes of meeting him).

I had no clue what to say, which was ok as he seemed uninterested in my response and launched into a 35 minute dissertation on Dr. Oz and urination output. Luckily my friend Dora was my wing girl and rescued me with an emergency call. I’m still not really sure what he was saying, but I am 100% positive that urination is not helpful first date conversation to have. Men take note.

15

Renato

Investors were still contacting me. I had eliminated or been offended by most, so only a few remained for in-person meetings. I met a nice capital venture man who was eager to get involved. I also had a Skype call with an hotelier who was interested in funding my dreams. The Swiss investor was scheduled to be in Miami, and I had arranged a time to meet with him there. It was always nerve wracking. I still didn't have a lot of business knowledge. I hadn't fully grasped the differences between, angel investing, seed funding, capital venture and private investors. There are a ridiculous amount of ways to get capital for a company, and I was still not only unsure of what I wanted, I was deathly afraid to take money from the wrong person. I also did not want to partner with anyone who didn't both share my passion to help divorcees and also allow me to run my company how I wanted to.

I received vibes from would-be investors that the minute I took their money they would try to railroad my vision, and me or try and micro manage everything I did. Neither of these I wanted or believed that I needed in my life. I had worked really hard to get to a place of independence, and I didn't want anyone controlling me or my company in any way.

Renato met me at a gorgeous hotel restaurant in South Beach. Just the atmosphere of sun and beautiful people increased my nerves and insecurities. I had of course Googled the investor and was astounded that he had heard of me or liked my company enough to discuss investing. I mistakenly wore a business dress, which was proving much too hot for Miami lunch time heat. I walked into the lobby and was immediately greeted by a tall handsome, greenish-gray eyed, Swiss gentleman, who in a very calm, reserved but confident voice asked how my trip had been. We exchanged greetings and were shown to an outdoor patio table, thankfully in the shade. Due to my nerves and the sun, I had begun to melt from the inside out.

He politely pulled my chair out, which reminded me how long it had been to meet someone so worldly or sophisticated. Renato was clearly one of the most intelligent men I have ever had the pleasure of meeting. His IQ was fascinating and I spent much of the meeting praying I didn't say anything too stupid or not right about my company. The best thing about him in person was that as successful and annoyingly brilliant as he was, he never once made me feel in any way less than he was.

I was impressed with his willingness to listen to my ideas and thoughts and validate them with his patient ability to educate me on the gaps in my business knowledge in funding and scaling of any company. He was one of the very few people I have come across, who has a deep-set inner alpha confidence, combined with a very empathic, compassionate personality. You rarely find this in a person. Very successful alpha men are predominately lacking in empathy and EQ. They rarely have the ability to be both strong and kind. This part of Renato was a revelation that there were in fact men who were walking versions of my favorite poem, "IF" by Rudyard Kipling. This poem personified how I wanted my boys to be and my perfect man.

I was sitting in the meeting as I do in much of my life with my mouth moving in conversation but my mind whirling on Warp Speed 8. I was contemplating how on earth did I get so lucky or deserve someone like Renato, to invest in my company? At one point during the meeting, Renato had very gently asked me what happened in my divorce and why I had been left in the situation I was in. It isn't something I generally discuss with people, but in that moment I felt safe enough to share a very little snippet of my personal story with him.

My words were met with the kind of compassion and kindness I have rarely seen in anyone, and triggered those tears that only ever flow, when you are being validated and shown that kind of kindness. I managed to change the subject and go back into hyper professional mode, but the truth is in that moment of kindness shown to me, I knew whom I wanted to partner with. I was just going to be ultra-cautious in seeing over time if Renato continued to be worthy of my trust.

We discussed life in general and he had a lot of great ideas and input about divorce generally. Sometimes it's just great to bounce ideas off people, and his worldly outlook and high IQ made for a great window into not only how he was as a global banking expert, but also into the person he was. Divorce had been hard on my heart and also on my soul. I had struggled and was still struggling to trust anyone. I kept very few people in my life after divorce and these few friends like Nancy and Dora had proved their loyalty over and over. Anyone new in my life had a huge mountain to climb, whether in business, friendship, or love, my heart was padlocked safely away and my soul was always on high alert, waiting for people to show me the worst in them, or their intentions. Poor Renato still had a way to go to prove himself to be trustworthy. He had on our calls and now in person, shown himself to be nothing but genuine, thoughtful, kind and trustworthy. But as all damaged souls will understand, I was going to need more proof, through consistency and time.

He walked me to my car and we said our polite goodbyes. It was amazing to me how my post-divorce life had evolved. I was grateful for this meeting, again grateful to the press that had connected me to Renato, and eternally grateful to the universe for thinking my idea worthy of this kind of high tier investor.

I didn't, in that first meeting, agree to terms, or investment from Renato. We both left it that I needed to put together a budget and compile paperwork outlining what I wanted and then how I would spend this money to take the company to the next level. I was not only thinking constantly about things I had never done, but I was also was also doing practical things I had never done before such as business plans, outlines, and budgets.

I was internally a much better new me. I was adding to my skill set daily and becoming not a wanna-be CEO but a real one, maneuvering through all the moving parts of this job title . It was incredibly hard work and time-consuming, and I often messed up things and had to redo them. But I felt a little more confident each day in myself and in the fact that I was somehow going to take this little dream and turn into a multimillion dollar empire and brand.

Date #35
Mr. Three is Better than One.

One of the more interesting emergences, relationship-wise, over the last two decades is the increased prevalence of alternative life styles, including swinging and polygamous relationships. I went on a date with a 50-something year old who ambushed me with it over drinks.

An awful lot of people believe that omitting information is acceptable in the dating world. It is not. It wastes everyone's time and is frustrating for both men and women when they show up on a date and see the person sitting across from him or her looks nothing like the photos, or that they are not single, or have some kind of lifestyle that wasn't disclosed up front.

The man spoke about a variety of things, before informing me that he was in a relationship with his wife and his girlfriend. Now, he was looking for a new girlfriend who might also enjoy being in a relationship with his girlfriend. The first thought that goes through my head is annoyance at not being given this vital piece of information. Secondly, I think this man must have some serious patience to deal with two women and now he wanted to complicate his life further by added a third! I can barely cope with one person and his needs, wants, and quirks. Who has time to keep more than one human happy, emotionally and physically?

Swinging seems to have become a pretty mainstream lifestyle. I have been pursued many times by seemingly happily married people, another thing that I think would be fraught with issues.

16

Best Insomnia Ever

I was happy with work, but my personal life was nonexistent,

I had been on dates, lots of them, but I had been unable to find anyone I felt connected to or worthy of rearranging my busy life to see. The holidays I had somehow muddled through alone again, and of course the sadness of spending them alone and being the only single person at my family's Christmas gatherings had felt as painful as ever. But I wasn't going to settle for a warm body; I wanted it all or nothing. I was still on the online dating apps, so at 3 a.m., when I couldn't sleep one evening in January, I was scrolling through match profiles when I received a message from a man with a profile but no photo,

I too had no photos up. I immediately thought who would not have a photo and send a message to another person who also didn't have a photo? It seemed very odd, but the message peaked my interest. It said, "You must not be able to sleep either. I don't know why, but I have a feeling from your profile that you would be very attractive and nice." It was 3 a.m. I was bored so I answered, "What kind of person messages someone with no photo?" He replied, "Someone with great intuition. Why don't we exchange photos and see if I'm right?

We exchanged photos and he was tall, dark, and handsome, I was apparently beautiful to him and went on to exchange phone numbers and texted the remainder of the night. He was smart, sarcastic, and unfortunately lived in NYC. This didn't seem to bother him at all, as he had a jet, as most of match people do. NOT!

My life was about to get a whole lot more glamorous, and my personal life was about to become almost as successful as my business life. I was living a dream I created through hard work and perseverance. It began to appear that the harder I worked the luckier I was becoming. Who goes on Match at 3 a.m. and connects with a tall, jet-owning multimillionaire who becomes smitten with you after a few texts? It was like a scene from a movie, and again came under the umbrella that truth is always stranger than fiction.

DD, let's call him, and I began talking every day, and within a week or so, it was agreed that we should meet in person. Being the old fashioned man he was, he insisted on coming to me first to meet here in my hometown. The Friday of his arrival came and after picking him up from the airport, we drove to the beach to spend the weekend there to get to know each other. I was relieved to see that in person he was as handsome and nice as he was online. It is a big gamble to let someone fly to meet you. sight unseen. Thank God for Facetime. It definitely helps in the online dating world.

We went to dinner at the beach and had a few drinks, a few laughs and our first kiss. DD was entirely alpha. You could see why he was so successful; I also on first impressions had the feeling that you probably wouldn't want to get on the wrong side of him. I had had a crazy week and as I often did, hadn't been eating properly. We woke up the next morning in the hotel very late for me, and by the time we ventured to get breakfast, it was almost ten am. The beach town we visited, like many in Florida, was full of chain restaurants and we ended up on a waitlist for a table at the Waffle House. DD and I had only met the day before and we were still in that weird, awkward getting-to-know each other phase.

We were seated at the bar area and as we talked about a multitude of things, including our plans for the day, I became suddenly and dramatically aware that I was about to pass out. I leaned into DD, muttered, "I'm going to faint," and swiftly proceeded to, with DD catching me right before I would have hit the floor.

As I was starting to regain consciences, I became aware that I was lying on my back on the disgusting Waffle House floor, with my legs being held up in the air, my arse hanging out of my dress and approximately five to seven paramedics and firefighters looking up my skirt while the one closest to my face, was asking DD if I was pregnant, if I had seizures, diabetes, and any known medical conditions. DD smartassidly answered that he had no idea, he hoped not and that we just met. As I came further to, I realized that DD was holding my hair and head up from the floor and trying to make me sip orange juice. I wasn't sure which part of all of this I was more mortified about - DD seeing me like this on the first meeting, the entire staff and patrons of the Waffle House watching me faint, or the firemen and paramedics seeing my naked bum in a pink lace G-string.

I refused further medical treatment as once I had sugar, I was feeling much better. We actually stayed and ate there. Then DD insisted we drive back to the hotel and I rest, instead of lying in the sun. I reluctantly agreed and found myself curled up on DD's lap while he stroked my hair and told me that he was now forever tied to me as he had saved my life, and that he would be expecting untold rewards from me after his noble deed.

I liked DD. He was probably more abrasive than most of the people I had dated. As a New Yorker, he had no trouble voicing his disdain. He didn't suffer fools kindly and he liked to scream at his various employees on the phone, which would have been off putting, but for that, towards me, he was very nice. We didn't have a ridiculous amount in common except that we both had three children and had one long marriage. We liked to discuss business, and he found me very amusing. But what we were both good at was doing things. DD was a man always on the go, I learned as I started dating him that he was not a person who could stay still. He liked hiking, cycling, walking at a very fast pace. He even ate fast. He got up at the crack of dawn and began work, and never finished work until he slept. He was a man on a mission. Which was both invigorating and exhausting over time.

Our relationship started off amazingly well. We enjoyed each other's company and intellect. We also were very busy. We would fly back and forth to each other, and our time together was filled with, dinners, sightseeing, meetings and activities. He was a good boyfriend, in all ways. The distance was bothersome but I kept reasoning that it was far better to date someone you really liked far away than to settle for someone close that you were not that into.

I could never figure out why, out of all the women in New York, he chose to date me. He clearly was a mover and shaker in NYC and could have dated a plethora of women there or anywhere. I was enjoying both having a boyfriend and also enjoying the fact that we got to do so much and that he wanted to do so much with me. I realized while dating DD that I hadn't really had a man in my life to do anything with since before my marriage. Even the simplest of things became super fun: a coffee-people watching, a wedding, or dinner was still so much fun for me as I really (except the 400 first dates) still hadn't had anyone to do anything with.

In my head, my almost year of dating DD was like a breath of fresh air. It restored faith in men, and showed me a new kind of relationship and life I could have with someone. It was much more fun and adventurous. A chance for me to get dressed up, whisked around NYC, and in a small way, feel like a princess for a little while.

Work was busy the entire first half of that year. We both loved our jobs and this was a common bond, because believe me, a lot of people have a hard time understanding how many hours and the kind of dedication I put into my company. DD got this, though, as he was used to doing the same. We had been updating website constantly but it was still having major issues, coping with the ongoing amount of traffic we were getting. Every time I thought it was ok, we would get some kind of national press that would spike visitors through the roof and take down the website instantly. After having a full two page spread in the *National Enquirer, USA* and *National Enquirer UK,* the website went down for two days. We literally couldn't get it to cope with the traffic. My lovely, kind school friend Matthew Carrington was photo editor of the Enquirer and had kindly got them to run my story, which today still probably is one of the only positive nice stories to run in that publication. I remember telling people I was going to be in it and immediately they asked what I had done.

It was becoming more and more evident that we needed a new website as soon as possible and that I needed funding as soon as possible too, which had become an internal struggle between wanting to trust Renato enough to allow him to buy in and wanting somehow for a miracle to occur that would mean I could hold partners off a little longer. Renato and I stayed in touch and met a few more times in person where I would update him on website figures and give him newly completed paper work to look over. DD at one point also had offered funding but, I was smart enough to know that unless he and I were headed for marriage, it was a sure fire way to cause issues between us.

The summer flew by in a blissful manner. I took my children to NYC, which I now had become fairly familiar with, and we spent a glorious week playing super tourists at museums sites and shows. We even met up with Nancy and her children for a few days to add to the fun. I had just returned from a weekend in NYC when I received a message on twitter from a casting agent. It still amazed me how anyone ever heard or found me. After a quick introduction, she asked if I would like to do a video audition for a major network for my own reality show.

Due to contractual reasons I still can't state which one. Needless to say, though, I was stunned that they even were considering me. An appointment was made and I spent a couple of hours being grilled in a video interview on all things DreamsRecycled and me. It felt a lot like therapy. They wanted to know my darkest moment, my funniest date, my goals, dreams, what I was willing to do, and what I wasn't willing to do on camera. It went well, but I still didn't have my hopes up. It seemed a long shot that anyone would want me to have my own show, not a show where I shared the screen with 12 other desperate housewives, or an existing show, but my own entire show.

It was amazing even to be asked to audition. A week or so passed and I was again in NYC with DD when I got the call that they wanted me to sign a multiyear development deal for my own show. I was shocked, ecstatic and also realistic. Unless I was green lighted, it didn't mean it would definitely be a go. I shared the news with DD and Renato and Simon who were all super thrilled. Nancy and Dora of course were shocked with me, and we used a long overdue girls night as an excuse to celebrate.

I was on a high. A great boyfriend and a bunch of contracts to wade through about having my own show, which I was nervous but excited about. There was no way I could pay for the kind of publicity that a reality show would bring. Add to that, an honest, savvy businessman who wanted to invest, and a user base that was growing every day. Another week home was followed by the day the contracts would be signed and another trip to see DD. Things had been busy that week and I must have missed something in DD's voice. He knew I was coming Friday. We had been having odd arguments that I put down to our insane schedules, but I was excited to see him and celebrate the contract being signed.

I signed the contracts at 3 p.m. and walked out on cloud nine. I was becoming the luckiest human on the planet, or so I thought. I met DD at the restaurant. He seemed off. We sat and he listened to my excitement as I told him the deal was signed. He congratulated me, but I could tell something was wrong. I asked him if he had a problem with me being on TV, for as successful as DD was I knew he wasn't a big fan of the limelight. He answered no that was great, but that he had something to tell me.

Since time began when people use either the phrase, *we need to talk* or *I have something to tell you,* no good will follow. I could tell from his face not only was it serious but really bad. A million thoughts of doom, death, disease, and illness flew through my mind. I imagined my self-telling him it's going to be ok and I would stick by him through whatever it was. What he was about to say though made no sense to me.

"I went for a paternity test on Wednesday." This is how it began, the speech. "I have a daughter. A baby. A woman I didn't know showed up at my office. I didn't remember her really only that she wasn't very nice. The baby looks like me"

My head began to explode. Questions tried to form on my tongue. I was hoping that he was going to somehow stop talking, or string some words together that would feel less like daggers of betrayal, stabbing through my mostly still bruised heart. A voice in my head screamed, *Not you DD, don't be yet another man to show me that you aren't worth trusting*.

I just sat there in a daze; I didn't even know what to say, so I said nothing. I stood up and began to walk slowly then faster and faster onto 34th street, tears blinding me, people watching as my face crumbled into a sobbing mess. My heels hurt. It was cold. I felt like I was trapped in some macabre tragedy where you are so close to getting everything you want and then some catastrophic event right at the finish line robs you of success and happiness. I kept walking. I didn't know where I was. It was dark. He somehow must have paid the check and caught up with me. I was in New York City. My bag was in DD's office. I had nowhere to go. No place to stay. And I didn't want to talk or hear any more words.

No more words, just shut up, I told him. He tried to hug me. I pulled away. People were watching. A lovers' tiff, I am sure they thought. It was much more than that, though. They watched as my heart and dreams shattered into a thousand pieces. My trust in DD, my vision of the type of person he was . . . I never once would have taken him as the kind of man who has sex with anyone he doesn't even remember. He went to church on Sundays, he gave to charities, he didn't cheat, and he never gave me one reason to think he would. He didn't flirt even, and it was one of the many things I liked about him. He seemed like a stand up, decent guy, someone who most certainly wouldn't accidently have a baby with a woman whom he couldn't remember and didn't like, he said.

I am not a fan of being a spectacle. I fumbled on my phone for the hotels.com app and booked the closest hotel to where I stood. DD kept asking, *What are you doing?* interspersed with *I'm so sorry*. I started walking towards the hotel. Tears reappearing at each new thought or word from him. I looked a wreck, I didn't care, I checked into the hotel. DD stood there, refusing to leave. I refused to speak to him because I knew if I did I was going to go ballistic. He got in the elevator with me, I walked to the room, and it ironically had a small picture that I noticed when I opened the room saying *doe a deer a female deer, ray, a drop of golden sun….* There would be no sun in this room, for me or ever again between DD and me.

We spent most of the night alternating between, crying, yelling, and silence. Questions flew out of my mouth, rapid fire at him. "Who is she? Did you cheat on me? How old is the baby? Don't you know how to use a condom? What kind of grown man is this stupid? How could you do this to me? Why didn't you tell me?"

He answered the way men do when confronted with crying, screaming, hurt females. Lots of denials, explanations that made no sense. He was drinking, he was single, he didn't know, he loved the baby . . ., every word cutting like a knife through my fragile heart. I had allowed this man to get close to me, to be the man to show me what being with a decent guy was like. The pain was insurmountable in that moment.

When we were in the room for the night, he even managed to kill off any of even the smallest hope that this was survivable by revealing that he had already made arrangements to have the woman and the baby moved to NYC so he could see the baby at will. Yes that was the end for me. I was in no way going to be a part of this Jerry Springer episode. While DD played baby daddy to some gold digging woman he didn't know and I lived five states away.

DD left in the morning. I had nothing left to say, I was numb and broken and again lost. A feeling of deep-seated pain and sadness gripped my body and mind. I looked for flights, but the only one I could get was later that evening. I checked out and spent the rest of the day walking around the city in a daze. The great thing about NYC is you can get lost there, you can disappear into the crowds, the Starbucks, the stores, the skyscrapers swallowing you and making you seem like a tiny spec of insignificant nothingness. It matched my mood.

I started noticing all the babies and baby things as I wandered, aimlessly killing time. I imagined DD walking around his penthouse with this woman he didn't like and a baby they accidently created. I felt sorry for him. He had no say in having it, but I was incredibly angry how stupid he was, and how badly he handled it. He had known of the baby for weeks before he told me. He had a paternity test because he must have suspected it was his. Omitting information is a form of lying although he would say it was to protect me. I didn't buy that at all.

I arrived that night back in Orlando and I have to say I was never more grateful to be home and as far away from DD and NYC as I could be. NYC had in one conversation gone from being a place filled with love and fun memories to the keeper of my heartache. I had no desire to go there again. My children arrived home a few days later, and I shared with them the reality show news and the news that DD and I had broken up. Tilly wasn't thrilled about this. She liked DD the most.

It was what it was, though. Another horrible reminder that the only thing that ever truly proves people to be trustworthy is time.

Date #68 #140 #207 #354
Mr. Angry Pants.

So, so many of these, they all kind of blur into one. Divorce has many healing stages, one of which is letting go of any anger you have towards your ex. If you have not reached the point of forgiveness, in my opinion, you are not ready to date anyone else.

Forgiveness is much more about your happiness and peace than the person you are forgiving. Anger, spite, and revenge only damage you from the inside out. Every one of these dates and probably another few, spent almost the entire date peppering the conversation with derogatory, hateful sentences about their exes, who were lazy, fat, whores, sluts, cheaters, liars, gold diggers, mercenary witches, you name it I have heard it.

Whether any of this is true or not, it's their issue, their karma. If the exes really did horrible, bad things or not, they have to live with what they did. Divorce means you are no longer tied, or have to concern yourself, with the persona or actions of your ex, unless it involves actual danger to your children. Let it all go. If they are wasting your money, having sex with your friends, dating twenty-five year olds, sitting around all day, spending money on their new flings, whatever your grievances are, let it go. It's the healthiest way forward for you.

It's also the fastest way for you to find happiness with another person. There is nothing attractive about hate, even if directed at someone else. There is also nothing attractive about bragging that you didn't follow the rules of the state and purposely screwed over your ex. No normal person wants to date anyone who acts like this. You are wasting a ridiculous amount of time and energy by still focusing on the past, if all that energy was channeled into a positive future and present, everyone involved would be in a much happier place.

17

Third Holiday Alone

DD and I breaking up had come right before the holidays and almost a year after we met. Ironically, I had been thinking and planning our first holiday together, but alas it was not meant to be, which meant I was about to spend my third post-separation holiday alone. It was the thing I dreaded the most. Something about the holiday season as a single person seems to amplify the feeling of loneliness. Whether it's the romantic family-filled holiday movies, or the family laden Christmas commercials or those damn annoying *Every kiss Begins with Kay* commercials, there are constant reminders that there will be nothing under your tree from a significant other.

Your family Christmas dinner will consist of your parents, your happily married siblings and . . . you. Holiday parties you will be invited to will be filled with couples, and you will show up with your wine and pray that there is enough of it so that you can keep smiling around your friends.

Luckily for me, though, this year, I had DreamsRecycled. It was my go-to happy place, my passion, and the thing that along with my children bought me the most joy. Since my return from NYC, and a long crying bitch session to all my friends, I had thrown myself back into work. I was aware that the more work I did, the closer to funding I would be and the better place I would be if or when my TV show was green lighted. I loved the thought of dreaming big and I had, over the course of the year, really got to a place of acceptance that this needed to be a global juggernaut of a company, not just a business to feed my children. I was ready for success, ready for funding, and ready to try to learn to be a better happier single person, not something that I by nature am good at.

I worked hard this holiday to try and stay out of the *bah humbug* zone.

It was around this time that I began to really start to shift my mind from thinking being single is a curse to that in many ways it could be a blessing. I have always been ultra-picky in whom I date or have a relationship. I by nature belong to the group of people who prefer to be alone than with anyone I didn't see a long-term future with. I think you could say I only date with intent. After the DD fiasco, I really wasn't ready to date properly again, and although I would window shop on dating apps at 3 a.m., still, I knew that my next few months had to be spent working on my company and myself.

There is that cliché that goes around the web that I, too, am guilty of posting, *If you don't love yourself you can't expect anyone else to*. I mostly don't like it as it rings too true. The problem with divorce is it leaves a residual that can easily manifest in an internal self-loathing or feeling of unworthiness. If your marriage was even remotely abusive, these feelings are often super-sized to leave you feeling, dare I say, unlovable, and sometimes worthless.

Being comfortable both alone and learning to fully love yourself again after divorce are giant stepping-stones you need to really fully heal. I was no different in this way, I had gone from Marcus to Simon to DD, and I hadn't really had a good chance or had the emotional sense to really find time to commit to working on myself. I knew I eventually wanted to get remarried but I wanted to know when I did find the perfect person for me that *I* was the best person I could be. Like all other epiphanies, I had since my divorce, I reached this one randomly and alone. I woke up one day with the holiday season looming ahead and just decided that this year I would enjoy it and enjoy being single through it.

I immediately, as is my nature, decided to plan a Christmas party for all my girlfriends at my house. My house had seen very few people since my divorce. I felt it was a place that needed to stay person free. Makes no sense, in hindsight, but at the time it did to me. I was once again going to put up the 12-foot Christmas tree and all the decorations that I had long since down sized to a little tree and a reindeer statue. I was going to bake again the dozens of cookies out of my Grandmother Lucille's recipe book, and it would once again be a season of joy.

We would start new traditions of new things that the kids would associate only with our new kind of family. This I did. I began feeling grateful for time alone, for options to go anywhere with anyone I chose too. I started showing up to parties alone, looking drop dead gorgeous and feeling great. Both happy about getting to show up and leave alone. I started saying yes to every invite, well as many as I could. And I went places with no expectations. Every place I went wasn't always fun, but for the most part, I had a great time. I flirted, laughed, lived and became more comfortable alone with each event.

I started to integrate the concept of being grateful much more heavily into my life. I was grateful for whatever the day had to bring, grateful for my children, family, friends, and company. I was grateful for the little things, the good song that came on the radio, the car pool mom picking up my kids so I could work, the way a certain dress fit, or a smile from a stranger. When you start to look at the world with grateful eyes, the world starts to look a whole lot better.

I began to enjoy Friday night alone in my empty house with takeout sushi and a bottle of honest Ice T. I started to treat myself better. Instead of waiting for an occasion or someone else to buy me something, I went ahead and spoiled myself when funds allowed. I bought the dress for my birthday. I started buying myself boots. I deserved them. I worked hard. They made me happy and as shallow as boots may seem, I felt great whenever I wore them.

I didn't need a man to give me things. I began to implement the rule of speaking more kindly to myself. I had long ago decided that there is probably truth to the saying *thoughts become things*. I started saying to myself that I was beautiful, I was enough, I was worthy, sexy, and smart. Sounds a little cheesy, but it certainly goes a lot further in your recovery process than standing in front of a mirror, condemning yourself as too fat, too thin, too ugly, old, whatever negativity we allow to crawl into our heads. It is extremely damaging to anyone's psyche.

We, of course, are own biggest critics, but we need to also be our biggest supporters. We have the power entirely alone to lift ourselves to a happier and more confident place. As nice as external validation is, this is not what should define us. I think I had allowed it to define me after my divorce. I had been overwhelmed with attention but this wasn't respect.

It wasn't meaningful, and although it bandaged my bullet holes at first to open a dating app and see hundreds of messages from men saying I'm beautiful, hot, sexy, stunning, etc. It must start from the inside first. If I don't feel inside that I actually am those things, then they are just words running off me like off a duck's back.

I was still working out, something that I had reigned in to be less obsessive. I was eating a lot healthier. A healthy body makes it much easier to get to a healthy mind. I had reached a point of understanding over those next few months that life really isn't about who you end up with or where you end up. Life is much more about getting to that place each and every day. Life is all about the journey, I tried to enjoy the ride, and the downs had made me appreciate the ups more. I stopped buying into the nonsense that the only way to be happy has to involve a man and two rings. The best kind of happy is actually not a future event. It is arriving at a place where daily, you wake up with a purpose, a smile and a grateful happy heart that you and you alone created. I had through a long learning curve got to this place and I was beginning to be self-accepting and happy on my own terms.

I had a great holiday season that year; I spent my birthday on a date with a fun, random guy. I spent Thanksgiving with a guy friend who showed up with wine. The Christmas party consisted of 12 amazing supportive women who were happy to bring way too much food, and even happier to deplete the giant vat of margaritas I had made.

My kids loved the new traditions of French toast casserole for Christmas breakfast, and the honey-baked ham and cheese potatoes I made for dinner. We ate cookies and watched Christmas movies back-to-back, snuggled in our living room and I began to think that this really was all so very worth it.

Date #139
Mr. I'm the only man to ever have a child.

I love my kids. I can discuss my kids with the best of parents. I, however, realize they are not better, different, or more interesting than anyone else's children. They all are gifted, all exceptional all in their own mix of things.

I went on a date with a man who spent the entire one and a half hours discussing his child. How fast the child ran, what math the child could do, how he had learned a song, on and on, insufferably oblivious to the fact that I am well aware how kids are. I have three, but even if I had none, I think the average person may find this kind of date strange. On a date, sell yourself not your child. The child will be happy if you are happy. It's as simple as that.

18

Let's Talk About Cash

When I wasn't working on myself and learning to be happy alone, I was working on DreamsRecycled. I finally managed to assemble all the paper work for Renato. He was in town and we were due for a meeting. He didn't know it yet, but I was about to agree to the terms and become his partner. We, of course, had been going through the motions of becoming partners. I had somehow managed to avoid actually agreeing to anything, part of me was still waiting for him to morph into something or someone totally different, as men seemed to have a way of doing around me.

He had, however, been consistent in everything he had said and done, no red flags, no left of center demands. Firm and fair, interested but not overly pushy. I had begun to trust him, listen to his advice, and calmly acknowledge that he really knew much more than me about business in general.

We met at a restaurant in Naples, Florida. He was as charming and sincere as ever. I gave him an update on DreamsRecycled's statistics. We politely discussed his family and travels, and he asked how my children were. We weren't even to the place of ordering food, when I blurted, "I am ready for funding, I want you to be my partner."

He started to laugh, and said we had better switch to wine to celebrate. He called over the waitress and ordered us drinks. Once they arrived, he toasted to our new partnership and added "Tiffany you have to be the hardest woman in the world to give money to." I laughed. Maybe I was, but I knew far too well how devastating one bad choice could be. Renato had proved himself to be a trustworthy person over that year. He had been patient, interested, showed compassion and a true desire to help our community of divorcees. It was a great meeting; I couldn't believe still that someone like Renato believed so much in my idea and me. He, too, had actually been extremely helpful in reassembling some of my broken pieces. Sometimes just having someone you truly admire believe in you is the greatest gift they can give you. Renato had done this for me, and in so doing, legitimized the value of the company and given it much sturdier business legs with him aboard.

Furthermore, in securing funding, my company had been valued in the seven figures, which of course for a startup owned, founded and conceived by a single mom with no skills, who had been deemed unemployable only 13 months before, was the definition of success! To have a global investor validate this was beyond my wildest dreams. The exhilaration, the personal inner happiness that you can only get from working your butt off to achieve something you really truly believe in is something that is almost indescribable. To say I was happy and proud of my self was an understatement.

I was following my calling. I had taken action from a simple dream. I had been resourceful *over* educated, listened to my instinct over any formal skill set, and this had got me to a place that others around me would never have believed I could have reached.

I was the startup *Dream Queen* and I was overjoyed with the company I had created. My little idea was after all going to become a global brand and, most importantly to me, I knew we would reach and help so many more "mes" who in their darkest hour really feel like I had - that divorce would be something from which they could never recover.

I ended 2014 with a large deposit to our business account, a happy heart, a lovely holiday, a reality show contract, and a new business partner. It was the coming together of a million working hours, hundreds of sleepless nights, a million tears, and a dream.

I had healed my heart through hard work, through helping others. During the dark depressing years I would have told you I wasn't capable of anything. I had somehow managed to achieve. I would have probably also felt that I wasn't worthy of any of it. Now I had accepted that I was just as worthy as anyone else of success, just as special. I mean this as in we are all special. There is no one more special or unique. We all are one of a kind. When you embrace the idea that anyone happy or successful isn't fundamentally different than you are, you can free yourself of self-doubt and comparisons.

Nothing about me is truly spectacular; I didn't have a better education than other people. On the surface I am pretty normal. I think that passion, belief in what you do, and hard work a lot of times outweighs talent or education. This is great to understand though as it levels the playing field. You don't need fancy degrees or be able to speak eight languages. You don't even need to know a lot about the business you wish to start. You just need the drive and ambition to dedicate yourself to learning about your field.

Effort also counts. It really does. Consistency and effort are always a winning combo, and with it, you can achieve almost anything you set your mind to. I had somehow managed to out achieve anything that I even thought was possible. I was a success, by anyone's definition, and I deserved it!

Date #59
Mr. How Does That Make You Feel.

I am still unsure of what was going on during this date. He seemed like a normal, successful, divorced father who was very nice. Maybe too nice. He listened intently to every word I said, asked sensible questions, yet, after every single answer I gave, he interjected the phrase "How does that make you feel?"

As the date wore on, I started to think he was kidding. It was extremely odd. "Tiffany, when was your divorce?"

"Few years ago"

"How does that make you feel?"

A minute later . . . "You have a daughter? That's great, Tiffany! How does that make you feel?"

Two minutes later. "You started a company? Fabulous! How does that make you feel?"

I'm still not sure if he fancied himself an amateur therapist, or if he was somewhere along the way told that women on dates like if you ask them how they feel. By the end of the date, all I was feeling was that I never wanted to see him or hear that phrase again.

Date #178
Mr. Cheater.

I am not a fan of cheaters. One of the more shocking revelations since my divorce is just how prevalent it really cheating is. It transcends sex, race, and religion. An estimated 87% of men and 67% of women admit to cheating on a significant other. I have been contacted and hit on by more men who were married (or in a committed relationship) than I can count.

The saddest of which, I think, was a married man who had his photos totally visible on a dating website. He had a very long meaningful description of how he wanted to find the one true love of his life. He was an older man who was an executive in some line of work.

I met with him a few times before I was told that, in fact, he was married to a much younger woman who he was very unhappy with. Turns out I was not his first date while married. He had also had multiple full-scale relationships with other women during this time.

In this same theme, Date #43 was, I am pretty sure, married. He actually sat through most of dinner, giving me a detailed description of every woman he had cheated on his wife with, right up to their separation. However, he assured me he would never cheat on me in a relationship, as I was different.

If you believe that any male or female will, in fact, be different than they are today, you are fooling yourself. You have no power to fix or change anyone. This was another hard lesson to learn for me regarding dating.

19

Girls Just Want to Have Fun

2015 stated with a bang. Receiving funding had enabled us to contract a new web team to totally rebuild the website and add on a slew of features and upgrades I had wanted for our users. We added a divorce directory of secondary services, better chat rooms, a larger overall marketplace, better geo locations for our ads, and a ton of other upgrades. It was a lot of work, but I knew it would be so worth it. Before I threw my self entirely into this, it was time for a little “r and r” and a girls’ weekend. Dora, Nancy, and I were headed to Naples for fun, sun and sand.

We packed up the car and started driving to the resort. It was always fun spending time with my best friends. They were excited that I had funding and were astonished as only best friends can be about the reality show.

“Of all the people in the world, why would they want you?” they teased. The girls had been there for me through the last few months of depression that had resulted from my breakup with DD. They, of course, were totally Team Tiffany. As we drove to the beach, we discussed the bad luck I had had with a string of men. The standing joke was that all I needed was a criminal to round out the full deck of misfits. They were still really the only people I confided my darkest fears to, I lamented that maybe I really was not meant to be anything but single. I shared with them, my concern that maybe I was responsible for having such poor judgment of men.

I had ended up back at the divorce lawyer office after being served with papers requesting more time with the children from their dad. Divorce really is forever when you have children. The last thing I had wanted to do was give up time with my children, or spend money, time, and energy on lawyers and legal proceedings. At least though this time, I found a really great lawyer whom I felt confident in using. DreamsRecycled had educated me enough to know the second time around how to better handle and cope with legal issues.

I had become far less of a doormat and far more of a fighter, even though by my nature, I am still very anti confrontation. Success in my business life had given me a new-found respect for myself and a new belief in my worth as a person. My business had given me a new identity and a concrete foundation to build higher self-esteem. It was empowering and refreshing to me, and I was almost giddy some days with happiness that I knew I alone had created.

Dora and Nancy got an earful on the drive and we arrived in full vacation mode at the resort, I snapped a photo, downloaded it to social media and thought nothing of it. We lay on the beach, sunrays soaking us, gossiping about all things, half of which will only ever make sense to us. It was what life was about, working hard for moments like this. Dora had me crying in laughter in no time and Nancy's laugh always tended to heighten our hysterics when we are together. I hear my phone alert and I see it's Marcus. That's odd, I thought. He rarely texts me randomly.

After our break up, Marcus morphed into a kind of male dating Yoda. He liked warning me of men like him. He was a good friend and someone I knew would be there if I ever needed him. I had actually called him on my return from NYC and he had offered to come over which I declined. Our dynamic wasn't very easy to define or understand but it made sense to us, and that was all that mattered.

I opened my message and it read, "What resort are you at? I'm here, too, and will be right over." I showed the girls. They had never met the mystical Marcus and were eager to see him in the flesh.

Within about 30 minutes, he showed up by the pool and bought us drinks, Marcus is one of the few people I know that no matter how many times you see him, you are always struck by how incredibly good-looking he is. He sat awkwardly close to me and we all drank and told stories until it was time for him to head to his business dinner and us to head to girls dinner. He hugged me a little too long and I could feel a shift in our dynamic, within his breath on my neck as he said goodbye.

During dinner, we were a buzz with a few too many cocktails. Dora never drinks but Nancy and I like to make up for it every so often. We don't get a lot of quality girl time, between our children, work and their husbands. It's often hard to coordinate spending time together. There was much talk about Marcus. The girls gushed over how handsome and nice and sweet he was. They commiserated with me that as great as he is, he and I couldn't date since he didn't want a relationship with me or anyone. "But you look so good together," Dora said. "Out of all the idiots you have dated, isn't he the best, truly? He may be a player but he's an honest one." I agreed but it was still like wanting something that doesn't exist. We headed to a club and danced until we grew tired and our feet hurt from the insanely high heels we liked to wear to girls night.

As soon as we got back to the hotel my phone started blowing up again. It was Marcus. "Where are you? I have been waiting for you to get back. I am in the bar downstairs." I was insanely tired and had no idea how I was going to stay awake. I threw on some workout clothes and left the girls to sleep. The bar of the resort was closing so we grabbed couple last drinks, asked for them in plastic containers, and headed outside to the beach.

I have lived in Florida a long time but I will never get over the beauty of the beaches. It was dark except for the moonlight bouncing off the lounge chairs and reflecting in the pretty calm gulf water. We found a front row lounger and pulled the canopy back up as there was a very slight cool night beach breeze. We lay on the lounger and he pulled me onto his chest. He smelled amazing as always, and in very hushed voices so as to not disturb the stars, we whispered our thoughts to each other. I had forgotten how lovely he was, probably blocked it out of my mind so as not to miss him. Marcus' inner calm and beauty outweigh his outwardly hotness, the combo though was undeniable wonderful.

We fell asleep that night, on the beach in a cabana. The respect and friendship that had been built over the last few years culminated in a sweet romantic evening. Under the stars and moon, without a soul around, we created our own little memory. We woke as the sun rose. He had to head to a meeting and I back to the room with the girls. There were no words spoken. It was mutually understood that as nice as that night was, it was just an encapsulated moment between two people who care for each other, yet would never be in a relationship.

I met the girls and we went to breakfast where, of course, as girls do, I shared the events from the night before. Dora and Nancy are great because they always want me to be happy. They are always rooting for me to succeed in love or business. Great girlfriends make you feel 13 again. It becomes all about, hair, clothes, boys, giggling and being silly. I do think this is an advantage women can have after their divorces. We have these kinds of friendships to take our mind off everyday life.

Date #37
Mr. Money.

Another odd dating phenomena has been the notion that women can be bought. I personally like to be treated like a lady. I don't mind when men insist on paying the check on first dates. I do, however, object to men offering you trips, money or shopping sprees to try and lure you into bed.

The old adage is so true that the right kind of woman wants respect, time and effort, not handbags. Mr. Money, after one date, spent months trying to buy his way into my knickers. It apparently works with certain women, and those women make it harder for the rest of us to get respect. Mr. Money never got another date, and I found his attempts troubling at best.

20

Dreams 2.0

We launched DreamsRecycled 2.0 in April 2015. It seemed at the time that everything was on the right track. Renato was supportive as ever, celebrating every advance we made. I had a great group of friends and family who were there to raise my sprits when things didn't go quite as planned. I was still mostly broke, as we reinvested all company money back into the company. As frustrating as it can be, even this didn't seem to bother me as much as it once had.

Divorce is the ultimate stress life event. We can be totally crushed and defined by it. If we let it crush us, it will. From 2010 to 2015 my life had been chock filled with uncertainty, turmoil, depression, disappointments and sadness. It also had been filled with discovery, progress, hard work, achievement and change. I put the change in the positive list because anyone who goes through a divorce has change thrust upon him or her. We can fight it and struggle against the tides of change, or we can float with them, onto new better brighter futures.

My story is very much to be continued, I have no doubt there will be many more triumphs and failures along the way both personally and professionally. I will not be defined by either of those, but rather by the way I choose to cope with them, by my attitude, my resilience and my positive outlook. I will continue to dream huge, set goals for global expansion in DreamsRecycled and aim for true unconditional love in my personal life. I won't settle for less than what I want and know I can achieve in both.

Before I started DreamsRecycled, I would have described success as a financial number. My divorce and adversity surrounding it was a rude awakening in realigning my priorities in life. DreamsRecycled is an astonishing success to me, not for the amount of money it makes or has the potential to make worldwide, but for the unlikelihood of one unemployable British girl who followed her dream with no skill set to be able to do this at all. I somehow found the true meaning of happiness along the way. It's a success because I found my passion, my true calling to help and guide other divorcees through this difficult time. We had reached over two million divorcees in the first two years. That is two million people thus far that we gave hope and validation to. That's my definition of success professionally - feeling good about what you do on a daily basis. Knowing that what you are working for is helping others.

In my personal life I feel ridiculously successful also. Not because sometimes I don't feel lonely, not because at time I don't have to deal with rejection and heart ache, but because I have come to a place in my life where being in or out of a relationship or marriage doesn't define me or my happiness. I wake up every day happy; I have stresses with work, children, and life. We all do, but these too don't define my happiness. I am far from perfect, I still cry, I still have crappy days or events, others still at times show us that the world can still be a cruel place. I however accept that the only control I have is how I react to these events and people.

I realized that as hard of a struggle as it was, and believe me it was hard, I wasn't good at the whole *choose to be happy* thing. It's a bit like eating healthy or working out. You know the results will be great, but it takes daily effort, thought, and commitment to get there. It's also like healthy eating as in some days you may fall off the wagon and have an unhappy day. You just wake up the next day, make another conscience effort to be happy, and start all over again. I daily CHOOSE happy. It's the single most defining thing that changed my life, realizing it is a choice, an action. A decision to focus and be grateful for all the good in my life and what I *have* instead of worrying about what I don't have. A belief that overall I (and most western world inhabitants) am afforded a life that is much better than most. I try to live my life being grateful for everything, including the mundane things we so often take for granted.

Divorce is the permanent severing of two people from each other's life. When we really accept the permanency of this and then strictly focus on the present, on our future, and most importantly, on ourselves, we get to a happier, healthier place more quickly. I was so drowning in the aspects of loss from my divorce that I had forgotten what I had gained. I could change careers, reinvent myself, wear sexy clothes, date anyone or no one, travel anywhere, and make out with my first ever boyfriend on the other side of the planet. I could spend weekends with multimillionaire boyfriends. I could start my own company. I could ignore all the naysayers. I could choose happy. I could take daily positive action. I could dream huge. I was in control of my outlook and attitude.

The world was at my feet and in my grasp the entire time. I created my own destiny. There was no need to spend two years in deep depression in my cocoon bed, with puffy eyes and a broken heart. There was no reason to feel ashamed or guilty about my marriage ending. We all get approximately 77 years on this planet. Only you know the inside of your marriage and also your heart and its happiness. You can choose to become the master of your domain, the master of your heart, your future and your contentment.

As of late, the website has been racked with technical issues, but we are forging ahead. Social media is growing. Our outreach has become amazing. I am being asked for interviews, podcasts, and speaking arrangements. Every time I get asked to do anything it still brings me a high. I have carved this incredibly rewarding niche from my own serving of moldy divorce lemons. I'm insanely grateful. I smile a lot, I feel joy, I love helping others and inspiring them to dream huge.

This year has flown by as years do when you are engrossed in a project you believe in. I am once again ready to date, I have retried a dating app. You would think I am a glutton for punishment, but really it's just that I am an optimist and haven't given up on finding true love. This is also a choice I had made, the choice to believe still in love. After divorce it's a difficult thing to do, to believe in happy ever after.

We have seen the happy ever after often turned into debilitating misery. We have battered and bruised hearts, and even sometimes we feel our very soul has been damaged. I still, though, chose to believe, I had to, divorce has shown me the worst life has to offer, but I still inherently understood that I deserve love and I have a lot of love to give someone.

I liked being in relationships. I wasn't going to allow one person or a few bad exes to rob me of my ability to love. No one should give that kind of power to any one other person. If you choose to give up on love and happiness, you have by definition let your ex not only win, but control your destiny and any chance of future happiness. No one should do this, and I most certainly wasn't going to. So Match.com it was once again, giving someone the benefit of the doubt and choosing to believe that maybe, just maybe, there was someone out there who I could be happy with. I had met someone almost instantly on reactivating my account and we were in the slowly-getting-to-know-someone phase of dating.

I am driving my car to Miami to see the man I have recently met on Match. We are spending a few days at the beach, getting to know each other better and to work on my tan lines. It is a clear blue-sky gorgeous day. The traffic is not too unbearable, which is rare in Florida,

I like long drives. They are an excuse to think clearly about life in general. My mind takes a virtual stock of my life. I feel great, happy, and healthy. My body has returned to the curvy woman I love to be. I realize I haven't passed out for a very long time. I am grateful for my life, the one I alone created. Everything is falling in to place. I have a strong master plan for DreamsRecycled. I have most of the marketing and business plans done for global expansion, I'm thrilled with the prospect of helping more people. My mind is running very positive lists through my head of everything we have accomplished.

My phone pings its annoying tri-tone alert. It almost scares me I am so deep in thought. I glance at the name. *That's odd,* I think. I open the text, my eyes double scan the words…*Tiffany, It's always been you!…* and just like that, I am once again thrown one of life's curve balls… only this time I'm a hell of a better catch …

Backward ☺

You made it, through my many musings, stories, and dates. I hope I made you cringe, because what is life without a few embarrassing moments? I hope you felt the sadness, because you will know you are never alone in this emotion. I guarantee you felt the pain of divorce and hopelessness, because it certainly makes you realize that this too shall pass. It did for me. It will for you. I also hope you chuckled a few times, because a life without a sense of humor is not a life I want anything to do with. And it's also one I am not sure I would have survived divorce with.

What really is my greatest wish for you, though, is to see that this all (moving from the desperation of divorce to the celebration of life) is doable. I didn't actually do anything monumental on my journey. I just took daily positive action and never gave up. I know you have this within you, and I want you to know that even on the bad days, when life throws you curve balls, when things don't go your way or you are treated unfairly, you alone, still every day in every way, hold the power within you to choose happy and to continue to work towards success.

Setbacks are part of that journey. Mistakes, which are my specialty, don't define us, or at the end of the day, dictate our happiness or success. What does is the tenacity to get off your bum and say *I will not settle, I will not allow the cards dealt me to define me*. Don't. Take those cards, rip them up, and align your mind to only think in terms of the positive and doable. I challenge you to set huge goals. Eat that elephant one bite at a time. And never give up!

I know you can and you will have the happier ever after we all deserve. It's out there, so what are you waiting for? Put down the book, and start! It really is that simple,

With Hope For All Your Bright Futures,

Tiffany Ann XOXO

Tiffany's Lemonade Recipe

1. Take a very large heaping of lemons, usually can be found in any aisle of adversity.
2. Use said lemons to really assess the kind of life that would make you happy. Adversity is usually the end of something, so focus on what it could actually be the start of. Are you passionate about something? Have you always wanted to do something, try something? What does your ideal life look like?
3. Take the of the life you really want to have. Make a vision board of it even. Assess what realistic small steps you can take towards that life, even if its baby steps. Everyone has the power to do something. Start immediately.
4. Be consistent in taking daily positive action. If you miss a day, make it up the next day.
5. Ignore naysayers, critics and all other negativity. Surround yourself with positive people. Most often those telling you that you can't do something are those most afraid you will.
6. Ask for help. It is OK to ask and especially OK to at times need it. Help can come in many forms: doctors, lawyers, therapists, support groups, life coaches, friends and family. We are not designed to be good at change. It's normal if you aren't. As far as business goals, ask for help here also. There will always be people who know more about whatever you are trying to accomplish. You will be surprised at how many people are willing to offer advice, help and support. Remember, chances are they started with little also and remember how this was.

7. Let go of anger, unfairness, and, most importantly, exes., Think of the quote "let go or be dragged down." Everything negative on your healing journey will always weigh you down and be detrimental to you in the long term.
8. Focus all energies on building your future and everything you, in fact, gained from adversity or divorce. Make a list of those things. Do not allow your mind to focus on what you have lost. Chances are it wasn't that great anyway.
9. Celebrate every advance you make towards your new life. Rejoice in the positive steps you have taken and take credit for you alone have achieved this. Well done you!
10. Speak kindly to yourself. Learn to love yourself above all else. If you don't love you, how will anyone else love you?
11. Learn to not only accept change but enjoy it. Every change comes with a silver lining. Look for it and use it to your advantage. Think of change as a springboard to success, because it is!
12. Define your success in your own terms. Far too often we focus on money and marriage as end goals. Success can be happiness, can be giving to others, can be being blissfully happy single, or exploring the world. Do success your way and never apologize for it.

If you use these steps I assure you that your lemonade will be the best darn sweetest lemonade you ever had!

Survival tips for your divorce

1. Know the despair and heart ache you feel are normal. The other over 2.4 million divorcees a year (USA alone) are not only feeling what you are feeling, but are just like you in most ways.
2. Understand that you will survive, that this too, no matter how dismal, shall pass. Hundreds of millions of divorces have come before yours and for the most part, we all survive.
3. Take deep breaths, because oxygen is good for your mind and body, and stress levels. Even better, go for walk, exercise and remain active. Exercise releases endorphins in your body that naturally make you feel happier and more hopeful.
4. Surround yourself with only positive people. Use divorce as an excuse to remove toxic and negative people from your life for good. Use your energy for yourself and your own needs only. If there is ever a time to be selfish it is now.
5. Travel, where possible, can be as simple as visiting a town near you or a new beach, or as exotic as a cruise down the Nile. It doesn't really matter what it is. What matters is that you have a change of scenery, a removal from your everyday life, home and work. A change of location often resets your soul and gives you renewed hope. it also often helps you think more clearly and be more hopeful.
6. Seek help, if you feel you need it. There are a plethora of experts, doctors, therapists, and life coaches who are there to help. If you have no funds for this kind of care, I recommend joining a free support group at your local church or a meet up in your area. There

is no shame in seeking help and you will find that most "helpers" in the divorce industry have themselves also survived divorce.

7. Try where possible to be unaffected by your ex's behaviors. Not easy, but the more we realize that divorce at the end becomes a business agreement, the easier it becomes to act from a place of fairness than a place of emotion. This will serve you better in the long run.
8. Have fun. This may be the last thing from your mind during your divorce, but you owe it to yourself to try and maintain a social life. See friends, go to movies, dinners, and parties. Date if you wish. Being social allows us to see firsthand just how much more is out there to enjoy in this life.
9. Look after yourself in practical terms. Get enough sleep, eat well, baby yourself when need be, and try not to fall into self-loathing. You are not a failure. Your marriage more than likely wasn't a failure. Usually there are good memories and children to celebrate from these unions. Focus on that. Don't allow your mind to place blame on you. There is no benefit to this negative thought process.
10. Know that there are a million new smiles, people, places, successes and joys ahead. The average person, in fact, will remarry or find new love within three years of divorce.
11. Always remain hopeful, create things in your life to look forward to. Nights out with friends, trips out of town, vacations, a new book to read, anything that brings you joy. Remind yourself daily that there is so much in life to still experience and receive joy from, be grateful for this.

I have spoken to thousands of divorcees and the best thing I can say is not one of them after their divorce says they are anything but happier long term after it. Hold on to hope that not only will this day come, but you in fact have the ultimate say in how quickly it takes to get here. It's not easy but choose Happy, stay positive, and know nothing, not even despair, lasts forever.

www.ingramcontent.com/pod-product-compliance
Lightning Source LLC
Chambersburg PA
CBHW071214090426
42736CB00014B/2815
9780998268620